Broadcast Journalism

Broadcast Journalism

Dibyanshu Kumar

Publisher
Kunal Pustak Sansar
Delhi-110053

ISBN : 978-81-88614-37-0

Publisher : Kunal Pustak Sansar
L–45, Street No. 5,
Shivaji Marg Kartar Nagar
Delhi–110053

Price : 750.00

Frist Edition : 2014

Type Setting : Editorial India, Delhi–92

Printers : Shiv Shakti Printers, Delhi–32

Broadcast Journalism (in English)
By **Dibyanshu Kumar**

Contents

Preface

Broadcast journalism is the field of news and journals which are "broadcast", that is, published by electrical methods, instead of the older methods, such as printed newspapers and posters. Broadcast methods include radio (via air, cable, and Internet), television (via air, cable, and Internet), and, especially recently, the Internet generally. Such media disperse pictures (static and moving), visual text, and/or sounds. Scripts for speaking to be broadcast tend to be written differently than text to be read by the public.

Radio was the first medium for broadcast journalism. Many of the first radio stations were co-operative community ventures not making a profit. Later, advertising to pay for programs was pioneered in radio. Later, television displaced radio and newspapers as the main news sources for most of the public in industrialized countries.

Some of the programming on radio is locally produced; some is broadcast by a network, by syndication, etc. The "talent" (professional voices) talk to the audience, including reading the news. People tune in to hear engaging personalities, music, and information that they want. In radio news, stories include speech "sound bites", the recorded sounds of events themselves, and the anchor or host.

The radio industry has undergone a radical consolidation of ownership, with fewer companies owning the thousands of stations. Large media conglomerates such as Clear Channel Communications own most of the stations in the United States. That has resulted in more "niche" formats and the sharing of resources within clusters of stations, de-emphasizing local news and information. There has been concern over whether that concentration of power serves the public. The opposition says that the range of political views expressed and supported is greatly narrowed and that local concerns are neglected, including local emergencies, for which communication is critical. Automation has resulted in many stations broadcasting for many hours a day with no one on the station premises.

Television (TV) news is considered by many to be the most influential medium for journalism. For most of the American public, local and national TV newscasts are the primary news sources. Not only the numbers of viewers, but the effect on each viewer is considered more persuasive, as described by Marshall McLuhan ("the medium is the message" in his book *Understanding Media*).

This book contains the fundamental and basic information of subject and the selection of contents makes it an appropriate book for the students.

—*Author*

1

Introduction

Broadcast journalism is the field of news and journals which are "broadcast", that is, published by electrical methods, instead of the older methods, such as printed newspapers and posters. Broadcast methods include radio (via air, cable, and Internet), television (via air, cable, and Internet), and, especially recently, the Internet generally. Such media disperse pictures (static and moving), visual text, and/or sounds. Scripts for speaking to be broadcast tend to be written differently than text to be read by the public.

For instance, the former is generally less complex and more conversational. Radio and television are designed to be seen and heard sooner and more often than is a daily or weekly newspaper. Broadcast "stories" can be written in "packages", "readers", "voice overs", and "sound on tape".

A "package" is an edited set of video clips for a news story and is common on television. It is narrated typically by a reporter. It is a story with audio, video, graphics and video effects. The anchor usually reads a "lead in" before the package is aired and may conclude the story with additional information, called a tag.

A "reader" is an article read without accompanying video or sound. Sometimes an "over the shoulder graphic" is added. A voice over, or VO, is a video article narrated by the anchor.

Voice-over is a production technique where a non-diegetic voice is broadcast live or pre-recorded in radio, television, film, theatre and/or presentation. The voice-over may be spoken by someone who also appears on-screen in other segments or it may be performed by a specialist voice actor. Voice-over is also commonly referred to as "off camera" commentary.

The term voice-over can also refer to the actual voice actor who performed the recording. The terms voice actor, narrator, voice artist, and announcer are all similarly used.

As a Character Device

In the 1956 film version of Herman Melville's *Moby-Dick*, Richard Basehart, as Ishmael, narrates the story and sometimes comments on the action in voice-over, as does William Holden in the films *Sunset Boulevard* and *The Counterfeit Traitor*, as well as John Mills in David Lean's *Great Expectations* and Michael York in a television remake of the book.

Voice-over technique is likewise used to give voices and personalities to animated characters. Among the most noteworthy and versatile of whom include Mel Blanc, Daws Butler, Don Messick and June Foray.

As a Creative Device

In film, the film-maker places the sound of a human voice (or voices) over images shown on the screen that may or may not be related to the images being shown. Consequently, voice-overs are sometimes used to create ironic counterpoint. Also, sometimes they can be random voices not directly connected to the people seen on the screen. In works of fiction, the voice-over is often by a character reflecting back on his or her past, or by a person external to the story who usually has a more complete knowledge of the events in the film than the other characters.

Voice-overs are often used to create the effect of storytelling by a character/omniscient narrator. For example, in *The Usual Suspects,* the character of Roger "Verbal" Kint has voice-over segments as he is recounting details of a crime. Other examples of storytelling voice-overs can be heard in *Gattaca, Blade Runner, The Shawshank Redemption, Big Fish, Moulin Rouge!,* and *Goodfellas.* Sometimes, voice-over can be used to aid continuity in edited versions of films, in order for the audience to gain a better understanding of what has gone on between scenes.

This was done when the 1948 *Joan of Arc,* starring Ingrid Bergman, turned out to be far from the box-office and critical hit that was expected, and was edited down from 145 minutes to 100 minutes for its second run in theatres. The edited version, which circulated for years, used narration to conceal the fact that large chunks of the film had been cut. In the full-length version, restored in 1998 and released on DVD in 2004, the voice-over narration is heard only at the beginning of the film.

The genre of film noir is especially associated with the voice-over technique.

In radio, voice-overs are an integral part of the success of the radio programme. Although the announcer holds the prestige and claims all the glory, it is the voice-over artist that is the real drive behind the show. One example is David M. Green's Summer Pow-Wow [1] and his voice-over artist, Tim Wray.

As an Educational or Descriptive Device

The voice-over has many applications in non-fiction as well. Television news is often presented as a series of video clips of newsworthy events, with voice-over by the reporters describing the significance of the scenes being presented; these are interspersed with straight video of the news anchors describing stories for which video is not shown.

Television networks such as The History Channel and the Discovery Channel make extensive use of voice-overs. On NBC, the television show *Starting Over* used Sylvia Villagran as the voice-over narrator to tell a story.

Live sports broadcasts are usually shown as extensive voice-overs by expert announcers over video of the sporting event.

Game shows formerly made extensive use of voice-overs to introduce contestants and describe available or awarded prizes, but this technique has diminished as shows have moved toward predominantly cash prizes. Voice-over commentary by a leading critic, historian, or by the production personnel themselves is often a prominent feature of the release of feature films or documentaries on DVDs.

As A Commercial Device

The commercial use of voice-over in advertising has been popular since the beginning of radio broadcasting.

In the early years, before effective sound recording and mixing, announcements were produced "live" and at-once in a studio with the entire cast, crew and, usually, orchestra. A corporate sponsor hired a producer, who hired writers and voice actors to perform comedy or drama.

The industry expanded very rapidly with the advent of television in the 1950s and the age of highly produced serial radio shows ended. The ability to record high-quality sound on magnetic tape also created opportunities, as has the proliferation of home computers capable of recording, often using inexpensive (even free) software and a microphone of reasonable quality.

Manufacturers will often use a distinctive voice to help them with brand messaging. Often retaining talent to a long term exclusive contract.

As a Translation Device

Voice-over Translation

Voice-over translation is an audiovisual translation technique in which dubbing is recorded over the original audio track which can be heard in the background. This method of translation is most often used in documentaries and news reports to translate words of foreign-language interviewees. In some countries, most notably in Eastern Europe, it's commonly used to translate all kinds of movies.

Voice-over Translation of Movies

A typical voice-over translation is usually done by a single male voice artist. It's fast paced, though fully intelligible, usually trailing the original dialogue by a few seconds. The original audio can thus be heard to a large extent, allowing the viewer to grasp the emotions in the actors' voices, as well as hear the actors' musical performances if the film contains singing.

The dubbing usually contains only a hint of emotion, as many of the interpreters have stated that they try to follow the narrow path between sounding monotonous and "overacting". A significant drawback of such dubbing is the ambiguity as to which character is speaking at a given time, as the interpreter usually makes very few changes in intonation to distinguish between different participants in a dialogue. Any text appearing on the screen is also read out by the interpreter.

Due to the imprecise nature of simultaneous interpretation, as well as the difficulties faced by non-native speakers in understanding foreign-language vernacular, idioms, and culture references, voice-over translations are often riddled with errors in translation. Dmitriy Puchkov has been very outspoken about the issue, stating that simultaneous interpretation should be abandoned in favour of a more precise translation, with thorough efforts to research and find Russian equivalents in cases of lexical gaps, and maintains numerous lists of gaffes made by interpreters, including highly experienced ones such as Mikhalev. However, others have commented that the creativity of good interpreters can make the film more enjoyable, though deviating from the filmmaker's original intentions.

In Russia

Called Gavrilov translation or single-voice translation, the technique takes its name from Andrey Gavrilov, one of the most prominent artists in the area, but the name used to refer to single-voice dubs in general, not necessarily those performed by Gavrilov himself. Such dubbing is ubiquitous in Russian-speaking countries on films shown on cable television and sold on video, especially pirate copies, and are sometimes included as additional audio tracks on DVDs sold in the region, along with dubbing performed by multiple actors.

During the early years of the Brezhnev era, when availability of foreign films was severely restricted, Goskino, the USSR

State Committee for Cinematography, held closed-door screenings of many Western films, open mainly to workers in the film industry, politicians, and other members of the elite. Those screenings were interpreted simultaneously by interpreters who specialised in films, where an effective conveyance of humour, idioms, and other subtleties of speech were required.

Some of the most prolific "Gavrilov translators" began their careers at such screenings, including Andrey Gavrilov himself, as well as Aleksei Mikhalyov and Leonid Volodarskiy. Their services were also used at film festivals, where Western films were accessible to a larger public, and allowed the interpreters to gain further recognition.

With the introduction of VCRs in the 1970s, and the subsequent boom in illegal pirate videocassette sales, which were the only means of seeing Western films available to the general public, the same interpreters began to lend their voices to these tapes. Many of their voices had a distinct nasal quality, most pronounced in Volodarskiy, which led to the rise of an urban legend that the interpreters wore a noseclip so that the authorities would not be able to identify them by their voice and arrest them.

Interviews with many of the interpreters revealed that this was not true, and that authorities generally turned a blind eye to them, focusing their efforts on the distributors of the tapes instead. This was also due to the lack of specific law forbidding the work of these interpreters, and they could only be prosecuted under the relatively minor offence of illicit work.

The three aforementioned interpreters, Gavrilov, Mikhalev, and Volodarskiy, were the leading names in film dubbing in the last decades of the 20th century, with dubs done by each of them numbering in the thousands. Many of these dubs were made using simultaneous interpretation, due to time constraints caused by competition among the distributors to be the first to release a new production, as well as the sheer volume of new films. Whenever possible, however, the interpreters preferred to watch the films a few times first, making notes on the more difficult parts of the dialogue, and only then record a dub, which also allowed them to refuse dubbing movies they didn't like. While each of the interpreters dubbed a wide range of films, with many films being available in multiple versions done by different interpreters, the big names usually had specific film genres that they were known to excel at.

Gavrilov, for instance, was usually heard in action films, including *Total Recall* and *Die Hard*; Mikhalev specialised in comedy and drama, most notably *A Streetcar Named Desire* and *The Silence of the Lambs*; while Volodarskiy, who is most readily associated not with a particular genre, but with the nasal intonation of his voice, is best remembered for his dubbing of *Star Wars*.

It is unclear why the term "Gavrilov translation" came to bear Gavrilov's name, despite Mikhalev being the most celebrated of the interpreters, though the popular nature of films dubbed by Gavrilov may be the most likely explanation. Other notable names of the period include Vasiliy Gorchakov, Mikhail Ivanov, Grigoriy Libergal, and Yuriy Zhivov.

After perestroika and the collapse of the Soviet Union, when restrictions on Westerns films were lifted, movie theatres, the state television channels, and eventually DVD releases primarily employed multiple-voice dubbings done by professional actors.

However, cable television and the thriving pirate video industry continued fuelling demand for Gavrilov translations. This period marked a significant drop in the quality of such dubbings, as the intense competition between the numerous pirate groups and the lack of available funds resulted in releases with non-professional in-house dubbing. This was further exacerbated by the death of Mikhalev in 1994 and fewer recordings being produced by many of the other skilled veterans of the industry, who pursued alternate career paths.

Numerous well-regarded newcomers took their place, including Alexey Medvedev, Petr Glants, Petr Kartsev, Pavel Sanayev, Sergey Vizgunov, and most famously Dmitry "Goblin" Puchkov. The latter is notorious for his direct translation of profanity, as well as alternative "funny translations" of Hollywood blockbusters.

Recently, the use of Russian mat (profanity) in the dubbings has been a great source of controversy. While many pirate recordings do not shy away from translating expletives literally, Gavrilov, Mikhalev, and Volodarskiy have all stated that they feel that Russian mat is more emotionally charged and less publicly acceptable than English obscenities, and would only use it in their dubs when they felt it was absolutely crucial to the film's plot.

In Poland

Voice-over is the traditional translation method in Poland. Althought gradually getting superseded by subtitles in cinemas, it's ubiquitous on television and DVDs (except for children's material, especially animation, which is often fully dubbed). The word *lektor* ("reader") is used to refer to the voice artist as well as the technique itself.

Voice-over is the preferred form of dubbing among Polish viewers, and attempts to introduce full dubs to Polish television met with viewer protests and ultimately failed. It's also preferred over subtitles; an opinion poll conducted in 2008 shown only 19% of Poles supports the switch to subtitling in television.

In Bulgaria

In Bulgaria, voice-over translation is also common, but each film (or episode) is normally voiced by at least four actors. The voice artists try to match the original voice and preserve the intonation. The main reason for the use of this type of translation is that unlike synchronized voice translation, it takes a relatively short time to produce as there is no need to synchronize the voices with the character's lip movements, which is compensated by the quieted original audio. When there is no speaking in the film for some time, the original sound is turned up. Recently, as more films are distributed with separate voice and noises-and-music tracks, some voice-over translations in Bulgaria are produced by only turning down the voice track, in this way not affecting the other sounds.

One actor always reads the translation crew's names over the show's ending credits (except for when there are dialogs over the credits).

Radio

Radio was the first medium for broadcast journalism. Many of the first radio stations were co-operative community ventures not making a profit. Later, advertising to pay for programs was pioneered in radio. Later, television displaced radio and newspapers as the main news sources for most of the public in industrialized countries.

Some of the programming on radio is locally produced; some is broadcast by a network, by syndication, etc. The "talent" (professional voices) talk to the audience, including reading the news. People tune in to hear engaging personalities, music, and information that they want. In radio news, stories include speech "sound bites", the recorded sounds of events themselves, and the anchor or host.

The radio industry has undergone a radical consolidation of ownership, with fewer companies owning the thousands of stations. Large media conglomerates such as Clear Channel Communications own most of the stations in the United States. That has resulted in more "niche" formats and the sharing of resources within clusters of stations, de-emphasizing local news and information. There has been concern over whether that concentration of power serves the public. The opposition says that the range of political views expressed and supported is greatly narrowed and that local concerns are neglected, including local emergencies, for which communication is critical. Automation has resulted in many stations broadcasting for many hours a day with no one on the station premises.

Television

Television (TV) news is considered by many to be the most influential medium for journalism. For most of the American public, local and national TV newscasts are the primary news sources. Not only the numbers of viewers, but the effect on each viewer is considered more persuasive, as described by Marshall

McLuhan ("the medium is the message" in his book *Understanding Media*).

Understanding Media: *The Extensions of Man* is a pioneering study in media theory written by Marshall McLuhan. In it McLuhan proposed that media themselves, not the content they carry, should be the focus of study — popularly quoted as "the medium is the message". McLuhan's insight was that a medium affects the society in which it plays a role not by the content delivered over the medium, but by the characteristics of the medium itself.

McLuhan pointed to the light bulb as a clear demonstration of this concept. A light bulb does not have content in the way that a newspaper has articles or a television has programs, yet it is a medium that has a social effect; that is, a light bulb enables people to create spaces during nighttime that would otherwise be enveloped by darkness. He describes the light bulb as a medium without any content. McLuhan states that "a light bulb creates an environment by its mere presence." More controversially, he postulated that content had little effect on society — in other words, it did not matter if television broadcasts children's shows or violent programming, to illustrate one example — the effect of television on society would be identical. He noted that all media have characteristics that engage the viewer in different ways; for instance, a passage in a book could be reread at will, but a movie had to be screened again in its entirety to study any individual part of it.

The book is the source of the well-known phrase "The medium is the message". It was a leading indicator of the upheaval of local cultures by increasingly globalized values. The book greatly influenced academics, writers, and social theorists.

Summary

Throughout *Understanding Media: The Extensions of Man*, McLuhan uses historical quotes and anecdotes to probe the ways in which new forms of media change the perceptions of societies, with specific focus on the *effects* of each medium as opposed to the content that is transmitted by each medium.

McLuhan identified two types of media: "hot" media and "cool" media. This terminology does not refer to the temperature or emotional intensity, nor some kind of classification, but to the degree of participation. Hot media are those that require low participation from users, since they foster detachment. Conversely, cool media are those that require strong user participation, since they urge users to engage themselves completely in their use. Radio, for example, is defined as a hot medium, since listening does not require complete involvement from the user. In contrast, television is a cool medium, since it requires more user participation.

McLuhan's Concept of "Media"

McLuhan uses interchangeably the words medium, media and technology. For McLuhan a medium is "any extension of ourselves", or more broadly, "any new technology". In addition to forms such as newspapers, television and radio, McLuhan includes the light bulb, cars, speech and language in his definition of "media": all of these, as technologies, mediate our communication; their forms or structures affect how we perceive and understand the world around us.

McLuhan says that the conventional pronouncements fail in studying media because they pay attention to and focus on the content, which blinds them to see its actual character, the psychic and social effects. Significantly, the electric light is usually not even regarded as a media because it has no content. Instead, McLuhan observes that any medium "amplifies or accelerates existing processes", introduces a "change of scale or pace or shape or pattern into human association, affairs, and action", resulting in "psychic, and social consequences"; this is the real "meaning or message" brought by a medium, a social and psychic message, and it depends solely on the medium itself, regardless of the 'content' emitted by it. This is basically the meaning of "the medium is the message".

McLuhan, to show the flaws of the common belief that the message resides or depends on how the medium is used (the "content" output), uses the example of mechanization (machinery to assist the work of human operators), pointing out that regardless of the product (i.e. cornflakes or Cadillacs), the impact on workers and society is the same. In a further exemplification of the common unawareness of the real meaning of media, McLuhan says that people "describe the scratch but not the itch." As an example of so called "media experts" which follows this fundamentally flawed approach, McLuhan quotes a statement from "General" David Sarnoff (head of RCA), calling it the "the voice of the current somnambulism". Each media "adds itself on to what we already are", realizing "amputations and extensions" to our senses and bodies, shaping them in a new technical form. As appealing as this remaking of ourselves may seem, it really puts us in a "narcissistic hypnosis" that prevents us from seeing the real nature of the media.

McLuhan also says that a characteristic of every medium is that its content is always another medium.

The impact of each medium is somewhat limited to the previous social condition, since it just adds itself to the existing, amplifying existing processes. Therefore different societies may be differently transformed by the same media

The only possible way to discern the real "principles and lines of force" of a media (or structure), is to stand aside from it and be detached from it. This is necessary to avoid the powerful ability of any medium to put the unwary into a "subliminal state of Narcissus trance," imposing "its own assumptions, bias, and values" on him. Instead, while in a detached position, one can predict and control the effects of the medium. This is so difficult because "the spell can occur immediately upon contact, as in the first bars of a melody". One historical example of such detachment is Alexis de Tocqueville and the medium of typography. He was in such position because he was highly literate. Instead, an historical example of the embrace of technological assumptions happened with the Western world, which, heavily influenced by literacy, took its principles of "uniform and continuous and sequential" for the actual meaning of "rational."

McLuhan argues that media are *languages*, with their own structures and systems of grammar, and that they can be studied as such. He believed that media have *effects* in that they continually shape and re-shape the ways in which individuals, societies, and cultures perceive and understand the world. In his view, the purpose of media studies is to make visible what is invisible: the effects of media technologies themselves, rather than simply the messages they convey. Media studies therefore, ideally, seeks to identify patterns within a medium and in its interactions with other media. Based on his studies in New Criticism, McLuhan argued that technologies are to words as the surrounding culture is to a poem: the former derive their meaning from the context formed by the latter. Like Harold Innis, McLuhan looked to the broader culture and society within which a medium conveys its messages to identify patterns of the medium's effects.

"Hot" and "Cool" Media

In the first part of *Understanding Media,* McLuhan also stated that different media invite different degrees of participation on the part of a person who chooses to consume a medium. Some media, like the movies, were "hot"-that is, they enhance one single sense, in this case vision, in such a manner that a person does not need to exert much effort in filling in the details of a movie image. McLuhan contrasted this with "cool" TV, which he claimed requires more effort on the part of viewer to determine meaning, and comics, which due to their minimal presentation of visual detail require a high degree of effort to fill in details that the cartoonist may have intended to portray. A movie is thus said by McLuhan to be "hot", intensifying one single sense "high definition", demanding a viewer's attention, and a comic book to be "cool" and "low definition", requiring much more conscious participation by the reader to extract value.

"Any hot medium allows of less participation than a cool one, as a lecture makes for less participation than a seminar, and a book for less than a dialogue."

Hot media usually, but not always, provide complete involvement without considerable stimulus. For example, print occupies visual space, uses visual senses, but can immerse its reader. Hot media favour analytical precision, quantitative analysis and sequential ordering, as they are usually sequential, linear and logical. They emphasize one sense (for example, of sight or sound) over the others. For this reason, hot media also include radio, as well as film, the lecture and photography.

Cool media, on the other hand, are usually, but not always, those that provide little involvement with substantial stimulus. They require more active participation on the part of the user, including the perception of abstract patterning and simultaneous comprehension of all parts. Therefore, according to McLuhan cool media include television, as well as the seminar and cartoons. McLuhan describes the term "cool media" as emerging from jazz and popular music and, in this context, is used to mean "detached."

This concept appears to force media into binary categories. However, McLuhan's hot and cool exist on a continuum: they are more correctly measured on a scale than as dichotomous terms.

Exploring Theories

McLuhan's theories about "The medium is the message", link culture and society. A recurrent topic is the contrast between oral cultures and print culture.

Each new form of media, according to the analysis of McLuhan, shapes messages differently thereby requiring new filters to be engaged in the experience of viewing and listening to those messages.

McLuhan argues that as "sequence yields to the simultaneous, one is in the world of the structure and of configuration". The main example is the passage from mechanization (processes fragmented into sequences, lineal connections) to electric speed (faster up to simultaneity, creative configuration, structure, total field).

Howard Rheingold comments upon McLuhan's "the medium is the message" in relation to the convergence of technology, specifically the computer. In his book *Tools for Thought*[1]

Rheingold explains the notion of the universal machine-the original conception of the computer. Eventually computers will no longer use information but knowledge to operate, in effect *thinking*. If in the future computers (the medium) are everywhere, then what becomes of McLuhan's message?

Historical Examples

According to McLuhan, the French revolution and American revolution happened under the push of print. The preexistence of a strong oral culture in Britain prevented such an effect.

Television is dominated by attractive visuals (including beauty, action, and shock), with short sound bites and fast "cuts" (changes of camera view). Television journalism viewership has become fragmented, with all-news cable channels such as CNN starting in 1980 and Fox News Channel and MSNBC in the 1990s.

Local Television

The industry divides television into local markets. Such markets are defined by viewing area and are ranked by the number of viewers. New broadcast journalists generally start in the smaller markets (fewer viewers) and move up to larger stations after gaining experience. The larger stations usually have more resources and better pay.

United States stations typically broadcast local news 3 or 4 times a day: around 4:30, 5 or 6 am, 11, 11:30 am or noon, 5 and/or 6 pm, and 10 and/or 11 at night. Most of their nightly local newscasts are 30 minutes and include sports and weather. Anchors are shown sitting at a desk in a studio. They read teleprompters. Reporters frequently tell their stories in live shots outside the studio where the news is occurring. Morning shows include more "soft" news and feature pieces, while the evening news emphasizes "hard" news.

News Jobs

Anchors (formerly "anchormen"), serve as masters of ceremonies and are usually shown facing the camera in a studio while reading unseen teleprompters. They are often in pairs (co-anchors) side by side, often alternating their reading. Meteorologists describe and forecast weather and show "graphics" (maps, charts, and pictures).

Any of those people can become the most recognizable faces of a station. Reporters research and write the stories and sometimes edit them into a package. Reporters are usually accompanied by a videographer at the scenes of the news. The latter holds the camera. That person or assistants manage the audio and lighting. They are in charge of setting up live shots and might edit, too. The producer might choose, research, and write stories, as well as deciding the timing and arrangement of the newscast. An associate producer, if any, might specialize in elements of the show such as graphics.

Production Jobs

A newscast director is in charge of show preparation, including assigning camera and talent (cast) positions on the set, as well as selecting the camera shots and other elements (recorded and live). The technical director operates the video switcher which controls and mixes all the elements of the show. At smaller stations, the director and technical director are the same person. A graphics person operates a character generator that produces the name keys (on-screen titles) and full-page graphics.

The audio technician operates the audio board. The technician is in charge of the microphones, music, and audio tape. Often, production assistants operate the teleprompters and cameras, and serve as lighting and rigging technicians ("grips").

Online Convergence

Convergence is the sharing and cross-promoting of content from a variety of media, which in theory might all converge and become one medium eventually. In broadcast news, the Internet is key part of convergence. Frequently, broadcast journalists also write text stories for the Web, usually accompanied by the graphics and sound of the original story. Web sites offer the audience an interactive form where they can learn more about a story, can be referred to related articles, can offer comments for publication, and can print stories at home, etc. Convergence also lets newsrooms collaborate with other media. Broadcast outlets sometimes have partnerships with their print counterparts.

Radio and Television Basics

Although all journalism should be a flow of information between the journalist and the reader, listener or viewer, in the broadcast media it is of vital importance that the reporter-through the newsreader or announcer-actually speaks to the audience.

It may be that you are broadcasting to millions of people, but you must write your story as if you are telling it to just one person. You should write as if someone you know personally is listening. Picture a favourite uncle or aunt, cousin or brother and imagine that you are speaking to him or her.

Your style must, therefore, be conversational and as far as possible simple.

Remember also that, unlike a newspaper story, your listeners or viewers cannot go back on the bulletin to hear again something they have missed. Nor can their eyes jump around within a story or a page searching for the information they want.

In broadcasting the words and sentences are heard once only, one after the other, and all the information must be presented in such a way that it is understandable straight away. This is often called a *linear* flow of information because it goes in a *line* in one direction

You must help your listeners and viewers by presenting information concisely and logically.

You must always remember that by switching on a radio or television set, the listeners are inviting you into their homes, their workplaces and their cars.

Write and speak as if you were talking to them as individuals, face-to-face.

In Practice

You should remember all you have been told about writing the basic news story. Be concise, up-to-date, stick to the main point, use the active voice, don't start with quotes and don't overload.

KISS

Keep it short and simple. You should not try to get too much information into any sentence. Although you use the inverted pyramid style of story writing, you may only be able to use one or two concepts (ideas) per sentence. You cannot get as much detail into a radio or television story as you can into a newspaper story.

You cannot expect your listener to understand the Who? What? Where? When? Why? and How? of a story all in the first paragraph or even the first two paragraphs. Although as a good journalist you should not leave any essential questions unanswered, you may find that it takes all the time available for a single story to communicate only a few basic facts.

It is often said that you could put all the words in a ten minute radio bulletin on one page of a newspaper. Stick to one or two key points per sentence. No sentence should be longer than 20 words, except in unusual circumstances.

Just as a mother feeds a child one spoonful at a time, allowing the child to swallow each spoonful before taking the next, you should spoon feed your listener. Give them one piece of information at a time so that it can be digested before the next piece.

Where necessary, split a long and involved sentence into two or more shorter clearer sentences, as you would in conversation.

Right: Japanese boats have returned to fish in Fijian waters.

They were banned last year because of an international row over net sizes.

Now they are back in the waters off Vanua Levu.

Wrong: Japanese fishing boats, which were banned from Fijian waters during an international row over net sizes last year, returned to fish in the waters off Vanua Levu on Monday.

It may take more words, but what good is the most skilful sentence in history if the listener cannot understand it?

It might help you to write short and simple sentences if you first try to imagine how the story might appear in a newspaper headline.

Once you have reduced it to the bones of a headline, you can put some flesh on it for radio and television. Don't forget though that, whereas newspaper headlines can be incomplete sentences, without words like *the* and *a*, radio and television news must be in complete sentences.

Look at the following example and notice how we take the details in the information, strip it down to the bones by writing a headline, then add words to turn the headline into a complete sentence, suitable for radio or television.

Information: *A contract for the construction of a new road between Madang and Lae has been awarded to a Korean company.*

Headline: Koreans to build new road

Intro: A Korean company is to build a new road between Madang and Lae.

Use up-to-date Tenses

The single greatest advantage of broadcasting is immediacy. You can inform your listener as an event is happening, or immediately afterwards, without waiting for typesetters or printing presses. Do not waste that advantage.

Keep all tenses as up-to-date as possible. Use the present tense or the tense nearest to the present and, whenever possible, use a continuous tense to tell your listener that a thing is still happening, as they listen.

Compare the tenses in the following examples. The verbs are in italics.

Right: The Prime Minister *says* he expects an increase in imports this year.

Wrong: The Prime Minister *said* he expected an increase in imports this year.

Right: Leaders of the main opposition parties in Fiji *have been meeting*.

Wrong: Leaders of the main opposition parties in Fiji *met* over the weekend

There is no room for words such as "yesterday", "last week" or "last Monday" in the intro of a broadcast news story. If the date makes the story seem old or stale, hide it down in the main body of the story.

Do not use Quotes

Do not use quotes in radio or television stories. If you want your listeners to hear the words as they were spoken, record them on tape and use them as *actuality* (the actual sound of something or someone, sometimes also called *audio*). This ability to hear people speak is one of the great benefits of broadcasting.

Also, quotes in broadcasting cannot work as they do in print, where the readers can see the quotation marks. It is just as effective to turn quotes into reported speech.

Bad journalists try to get round this rule by using the words "quote" and "unquote" at the beginning and end of direct quotes. This sounds clumsy. It is much better in radio to rewrite quotes in reported speech. Compare the following sentences:

Right: The chairman said it was a crying shame.

Wrong: The chairman said: "It is a crying shame."

Wrong: The chairman said, quote: It is a crying shame-unquote.

If you feel the need to stress a certain word or phrase in reported speech, to emphasise that these are the actual words used, underline them so the newsreader can add the stress with their voice. Again, it is better to use actuality where possible. Some journalists mistakenly think that they will be safe from defamation if they add "quote... unquote" around danger words. In law, it does not matter whether words are in quotes or reported speech; they could still be defamatory. The only time you would use quotes in television is when you present them as text on screen. This most commonly happens when it is important the viewer can see the exact words used, for example in quoting a judge from a court case where audio or actuality of his voice is not available. These quotes are usually kept very short and given in large, easy-to-read type, punctuated as they would be in print media.

Put Attribution First

Attribution in radio and television goes at the front of a sentence, as it would if you were talking to that favourite aunt. This is unlike traditional newspaper style, which commonly puts attribution such as *he said* at the end of the sentence, after the quote. In newspapers, readers can see both the quote and the attribution together. In radio and television, your listeners need to know who was speaking before they can judge what was said. Remember the *linear* structure of broadcast news.

Compare the following sentences. The attribution is in italics.

Right: *A senior government economist* says that people in Papua New Guinea are paid too much.

Wrong: People are paid too much in Papua New Guinea, *a senior government economist* said last night.

By putting the attribution up front, you are also making your sentence more active, important for broadcast news.

Avoid Unfamiliar Words

If a newspaper reader does not understand a word, he or she can return to it and maybe look it up in a dictionary before proceeding to the rest of the story. Your listeners cannot do this.

By the time they have worked out the meaning of an unfamiliar word, the story will be over and they will have missed all the other details.

If you have to use an unfamiliar word or name, you must not hit your listeners with it without warning. You should never put it as the first word in your paragraph, but work your way towards it over familiar ground.

In the following examples, the unfamiliar words are in italics.

Right: In Mexico, the volcano *Popocatepetl* has erupted again.

It showered lava and ash for 50 kilometres around.

Wrong: *Popocatepetl*, a volcano in Mexico, erupted again yesterday, showering lava and ash on the ground over a radius of 50 km.

People's names can cause problems too, unless they are familiar. For example, the name of your Prime Minister or President may not cause problems, but an unfamiliar name might, as in the following example:

Right: A school inspector in the East Sepik says teachers don't listen enough to their students.

The inspector, *Mr. Arianthis Koloaloa*, says...

Wrong: *Mr. Arianthis Koloaloa*, a school inspector in the East Sepik, has criticised teachers for not listening to their students.

Repeat Important Words

Because radio and television listeners do not pay attention all the time, and because people often switch on their sets half-way through a bulletin, it is important that you repeat the essential features several times in the story. They might be half-listening to the radio or TV until something-perhaps a word relevant to them or their interest-triggers their attention. They then 'tune in' with their mind but, because of the linear nature of broadcast news, they cannot go back and retrieve any words they have missed. So repeat important words at least once in the story. In the following example, the words *Korean*, *Madang*, *Lae* and *road* are repeated:

A *Korean* company is to build a new *road* between *Madang* and *Lae*.

They estimate it will cost more than one-hundred-million kina.

Work on the new *Madang* to *Lae road* should begin in August.

The Prime Minister, Mr. Rabbie Namaliu, says the *Koreans* were awarded the *road* contract because of their years of experience.

Of course, too much repetition can be boring, so do not overdo it. A simple tip is to cover the intro and see whether or not you can still understand the story from what is left. Try it with the example above.

Keep Punctuation Simple

Keep punctuation as simple as possible. In broadcast news, punctuation marks are not only there for grammatical reasons. They also give the newsreader clues on breathing.

In general, the only punctuation marks you need are the full stop, comma, question mark and dash. Some writers like to use a series of dots to denote a pause, as in the following example:

The Prime Minister... speaking at a business lunch... said the economy is looking brighter.

Where two words go together to form a single concept, hyphenate them whether or not it is grammatically correct to do so. For example, write *mini-market*, *winding-rope*, *pocket-book*.

Simplify Numbers

Numbers should be included to inform, not to confuse-either the newsreader or the listener. Wherever there is the possibility of confusing the newsreader, write the number in full.

Right: two-million, nine-hundred-and-eighty thousand, and two.

Wrong: 2,980,002

Better still, round off large figures, so that the example above becomes "almost three million". This simplifies matters for both the newsreader and the listeners. The same rule applies to fractions. Write them in full, for example *one-half, three-quarters* etc.

With money, spell out the units, so that $1.50 becomes "one-dollar-fifty". Many newsreaders even prefer the date to be spelt out, as in the following:

Right: The 1st of March, 2007.

Wrong: March 1, 2007.

Avoid Abbreviations

As a general rule, avoid abbreviations. You can, of course, use "Mr.", or "Mrs" in your script, but do not abbreviate other titles.

Where the initials of an organisation are read as a word, write them as such, for example Nato, Asean, Apec.

But if they must be read individually, separate each letter with a dot, as in U.N., P.N.G. or Y.M.C.A.. Some broadcasters prefer to hyphenate the letters, to make it even clearer that they must be read out separately, for example P-N-G.

The first reference must be written in full unless the initials are widely understood on their own-as are the three examples above.

Do not use the abbreviations a.m. or p.m. There is always a better way which tells your listeners much more. Phrases like "this morning" or "tomorrow afternoon" mean much more to most listeners.

Right: The rocket was launched at three this morning.

Wrong: The rocket was launched at 3 a.m. today.

Give a Guide to Pronunciation

Pronunciation is a very large field. Most newsrooms should have a pronunciation guide for place names and other difficult foreign words. Good dictionaries should give you correct pronunciations, but if you are in doubt, check with a senior journalist or someone who is likely to know the correct pronunciation. For example, if it is the name of a species of fish, check with a fisheries officer.

When writing an unfamiliar word for the newsreader, make their task as simple as possible by writing it phonetically. For example, the state of *Arkansas* should be written as ARK-en-sor; the French word *gendarme* becomes JON-darm, placing the stress on the syllable in capital letters.

Do everything you can do to make the message clearer.

Writing for Television

Although most of the rules for broadcast writing (such as KISS) apply to both radio and television, there are a few additional factors to remember when writing for television.

Making television news is a more complicated process than producing radio news-which can often be done by one person. Television always involves several people, performing specialist tasks such as camera operating, scriptwriting, bulletin presenting, directing, studio managing, lighting and sound mixing.

Television also involves two simultaneous methods of presenting information-sound and vision. Of the two, vision is usually the most effective in giving details quickly. For example, you could take several minutes to describe a crash scene which can be understood from a ten-second film segment.

The words in television usually support the pictures, not the other way round. That is why television reporters usually write their scripts after they have edited the videotape (or film). You usually have to write your script so that the words match the pictures which are on the screen. This requires good language skills, especially in simplifying complex language. If a newsreader has to read your script live-perhaps from an autocue-it will help them if you keep the words and grammar simple and the sentences short. (An autocue – also called a *teleprompter*-is a device which projects a magnified image of the script on a clear screen in front of the camera lens, in such a way that only the presenter can see it. It is invisible to the viewers at home. It is used so presenters do not need to keep looking down at their scripts.)

Of course, the words become more important when there are no pictures to illustrate the story, only the sight of the newsreader's head and shoulders. But you should always try to think of ways of presenting some of your information visually, otherwise you are wasting half of your resources (the vision). For example, if you are telling about a new tax on beer, you will probably simultaneously show pictures of a brewery and of beer being produced and consumed. You might also want to show a graph showing how beer sales and taxes have increased over the past few years. And you may want a clip of the relevant minister explaining why he is increasing the tax.

As well as being aware of how your words will support the pictures, you must also consider the effect the pictures will have on your viewers' ability to listen to the words. For example, if you have some very dramatic pictures of an explosion, you should not write your script in such a way that the important facts are given while viewers have all their attention on the picture.

Perhaps leave a couple of seconds without any commentary during the explosion, then bring your viewers' attention back to the words gradually. Remember that every time you change the picture on the screen, your viewers' attention is distracted away from the words while they concentrate on the new image. Bear this in mind when writing your script to fit the edited pictures.

Because television viewers have to concentrate on both sight and sound, you cannot expect them to concentrate on lots of details while there are interesting pictures on the screen. So if you want to give some very important details, either do it when the camera returns to a picture of the newsreader, or do it through graphics such as maps, diagrams, graphs or tables or through captions.

Captions

The names and titles of speakers are usually written on the screen in captions. These must be simple and clear, so that your viewers do not have to spend much time reading them. Remember too that your viewers may not all be able to read. If you know that literacy rates are low among your audience, putting the written word on the screen will not alone explain essential details. For example, in countries with high literacy rates, television newsreaders or reporters use only captions to identify speakers. You may need to both present a caption and also read the name aloud.

Subtitles

Subtitles are text versions of the spoken words in the bulletin or program. They usually run along the bottom of the screen so viewers can read them while still watching the pictures and listening to the words being spoken. They are mainly used for two reasons: to assist viewers who have hearing difficulties (called *closed captions*) or to translate words in languages other than the language of broadcast. They generally need to be prepared beforehand and they require concentration from the viewer, so they should be done professionally if possible.

To avoid having to use subtitled translations of words spoken in another language, it is possible to over-dub what the speaker is saying by fading down the original sound and getting another voice to read a translation over it, either a fellow journalist or a professional voice actor. Simpler still is to fade down the words being spoken so they can barely be heard then the newsreader (or reporter) can summarise what is said in reported speech.

Stand-ups

One final word about writing for stand-ups. These are the times when a reporter speaks directly into the camera at the scene of the story. Each stand-up segment in news is normally about 10 or 20 seconds long, meaning that it can contain several sentences of spoken word. Some reporters write the words they will say in sentences on a notebook then read them out in front of the camera. However, this means that the reporter cannot look into the camera while also looking down to read from the notebook.

It is better either to memorise the sentences then put the notebook to one side or to remember only the key words you want to use then speak sentences directly into the camera. In both cases, it helps if you keep the language simple and your sentences short. You must also avoid using words which might be difficult to pronounce. If you try to say "The previous Prime Minister passed away in Papeete", you will get into difficulties because of all the "p" sounds. Rewrite the sentence as "The last Prime Minister died in Papeete."

To Summarise:

Follow these simple writing rules:

- KISS-keep it short and simple
- Do not use quotes on radio or in television scripts
- Avoid unfamiliar words
- Repeat important words
- Keep punctuation simple
- Simplify numbers
- Avoid abbreviations
- Show how to pronounce difficult words

Radio and Television Bulletins

All your work as a broadcast journalist leads ultimately to one thing-the time when your listeners hear what you have produced. This can be the news bulletin or a current affairs program. You have to use your on-air time effectively.

Although we will concentrate in this section on producing bulletins for radio, you can use similar techniques for television. The main difference is that television bulletins also include pictures, which have to be coordinated with the script. If you can understand the principles of producing radio bulletins, you can use them for television, adapting them to the style of your particular newsroom.

The Principles of Bulletin Preparation

Radio bulletins are usually made up from three types of material:

- written stories in the form of a script;
- voice reports from journalists, either recorded or live;
- recorded sound called actuality. This is usually the sound of someone speaking, perhaps taken from an interview or a speech. A short segment of actuality is called a grab. Grabs are used in a similar way to quotes in a newspaper story. In some countries, grabs are called cuts or inserts.

Preparing a bulletin should not be difficult if you remember the basic principles of news reporting. Remind yourself of the criteria for what is news: Is it new, unusual, interesting, significant and about people?

Each of these criteria will help you to decide what stories you should include in your bulletin and where you should place them within your five, 10 or 15 minutes. It is usual to give the most important story first and the least important story last. If you are putting together your first bulletin, stick to this technique.

However, once you feel confident that you can put together a simple bulletin, you can start to consider some extra factors which will change it from a list of stories to a proper bulletin.

The two main factors you have to consider are the overall order or balance of the bulletin and the pace of it.

Balance

Try to avoid seeing the bulletin simply as a collection of individual, self-contained stories. If you put a string of economic stories (however important) at the start of the bulletin, you risk losing your listeners' interest. They expect a balance of items, some heavy and some light, some about major political events and some about ordinary people. Of course, the actual mix of stories, their tone and pace of delivery will depend to a degree on the format of your station; serious national broadcasters tend to use more serious stories, delivered in a more deliberate style whereas youth-oriented music station bulletins might be lighter and brighter with more stories about popular culture.

Whatever your station format, your ranking of stories in order in the bulletin will give your listeners some indication of how important you consider each story. But there is some freedom within bulletins to re-order stories to add variety and balance to the bulletin as a whole.

Pace

You must also get the right pace of stories through your bulletin. By pace we mean the length and tone of a story as it appears to the listeners.

Some stories have a fast pace. The report of a fire, for example, will usually be written in short sentences, using short snappy words to convey simple ideas. It will have a fast pace. By comparison, a story explaining some involved political controversy may need slightly longer sentences with words expressing more complicated ideas. The story itself may need to be slightly longer. The whole effect is one of a slower pace.

Too many long complicated stories will slow the pace of the whole bulletin and allow the attention of your listeners to wander. Too many short, sharp stories may leave listeners confused, unable to keep up with the pace of changing stories.

Your ideal bulletin will have a steady pace throughout to maintain interest, with variations in pace during certain sections; slower at times to let your listeners catch their breath or faster at other times to pick up their lagging interest.

How do you achieve balance and pace in practice? You should rank your stories in order of importance then look at the order afresh, to see that you have a good balance of items and variations in pace.

You may decide that your most important three stories are all rather serious political stories about taxation, health insurance and an internal party squabble. Ask yourself: "What will my listeners think of three minutes of this at the start of the bulletin?" If you think they will be bored, what about putting the report of a street fight up to the third place in the bulletin, to inject some pace into that section? This may force your party argument story into fourth place, but you will now be giving it new life by changing pace after the street fight story.

Structuring the Bulletin

Now you understand the basic principles behind building a news bulletin, you can start thinking about how the stories and components such as headlines and actuality can fit. Bulletins are the broadcasting equivalent of a page on a newspaper, except that in radio and television you are more limited in where you place the different parts because, as we know, news bulletins are linear, therefore all the elements must be placed along the line of time so they are used most effectively.

Starting the Bulletin

The start is the most important part of any radio bulletin. It determines whether or not your listeners will stay tuned. Just as the intro is the most important part of a news story, the lead item is the most important one in the bulletin. If your listeners find this boring, they will assume that there is nothing better to come and go out to dig the garden.

If you are faced with a choice between two stories of equal strength for your bulletin lead, choose the story which is more dramatic. If your obvious lead story is rather dull, you should write it in such a way as to add life. Keep the sentences short, the ideas clear and simple. Although you should try to write every story well, you should give special attention to your lead story. This is the one by which listeners will judge the bulletin.

Headlines

Once you have decided on the order of stories, you should write some headlines for the bulletin. It is usual to start a long bulletin by headlining the major stories. This may not be necessary for a short, three-minute bulletin, but for longer bulletins your listeners will want to know what kind of stories they can expect. Your listeners will use the headlines to judge whether or not the bulletin is worth listening to, so write your headlines to promote the stories in the most powerful way possible.

It is good practice to headline the first two or three most important stories, and also one or two dramatic stories which come later in the bulletin. Many stations also like to headline the final story, on the assumption that, if they make the headline attractive enough, listeners will stay tuned to the entire bulletin until they hear that story.

You should write headlines for dramatic stories in such a way that you hint at the drama without giving away all the details. Remember that if you tell everything in the headlines, listeners have no need to hear the rest of the bulletin.

In English bulletins, headlines do not have to be grammatically complete. They can be more like newspaper headlines, stripped down to the main words. The following are examples of possible headlines:

- "More trouble for the Asean alliance."
- "Twelve die in a mine blast."
- "Why Russia is angry with Israel."

When writing headlines about announcements or humorous stories, it is best to be mysterious, to keep the real information secret until the listeners hear the story itself. Such headlines are sometimes called teasers, because the tease the listeners' interest.

For example, if you have a story about rising petrol prices, you might write the headline "Motorists face another shock at the petrol pumps". Never write the headline "Petrol is to rise by 10 cents a litre"-that gives the whole story away, and your listener can now tune to another station's bulletin or go and dig the garden again.

Closing Stories

Sometimes called tail-enders, closing stories are almost as important as lead stories. They are the last stories your listeners will hear and remember from the bulletin. You need to choose them carefully.

However, because many listeners do not maintain their attention throughout the whole bulletin, you should not keep your best stories to the end.

Light or funny stories make the best tail-enders. They add relief and a change of pace to heavy bulletins. They should be written in a more informal way than other stories, possibly with a play on words which your listeners will appreciate.

It is usual in English radio bulletins to signal the light tail-ender with the words "And finally...", as in the following example:

And finally, police in Apia are looking for a thief who broke into a house last night... and left his trousers behind.

Be careful, though. Humorous stories may not be appropriate if the rest of the bulletin is dominated by a major tragedy.

Closing Headlines

With longer bulletins, you can use closing headlines to remind your listeners of stories they may (or may not) have heard 10 minutes earlier.

Again they should be the major stories of the bulletin, excluding the tail-ender, which they should have just heard anyway. Unlike opening headlines, which should attract your listeners to listen to the bulletin, closing headlines are simply there as a service, especially to listeners who may have tuned in late.

Each closing headline should be a summary of the main point of the story, written in one sentence. Any longer and they become a repeat of the story itself. Do not simply repeat the opening headline or intro of each story as a closing headline. This is laziness which does not serve your listeners. Never repeat teasers as closing headlines: give the details.

Closing headlines are usually introduced with a phrase like: "Now to summarise the main stories,..."

Actuality

Short grabs of actuality are a useful part of news bulletins, for a number of reasons: They can often tell the story more effectively than a script. If your story is about a violent protest outside an embassy, a 10-second grab of demonstrators chanting and shouting will convey the atmosphere better than any words.

They can add variety to the pace of the bulletin, breaking up a long section of reading by one voice. On the practical side, they allow the newsreader to take a 30 or 40 second rest.

They are often a chance to let people within your community speak on the radio. People like to hear their own voice on radio occasionally, or the voices of people they know.

Using a grab of someone speaking can convince listeners that the person really did say a certain thing. They might not believe your report that the Government is resigning. When they hear the Prime Minister announcing it, they have to believe.

Actuality grabs should be kept short (between 20 and 40 seconds), clear and well-edited. A minute-long grab of a dull voice will slow the pace of your bulletin and may force listeners to switch off.

Grabs must be introduced, stating clearly who will be speaking. You only need to identify a person after paying the actuality (called back-announcing) if the grab is long and the voice is not familiar.

Grabs in languages other than your own should be overdubbed with a translation. This means that you fade down (reduce) the sound of the original speaker until it can only just be heard, then play the voice of the translator over it. You can occasionally use grabs in languages other than your own without overdubbing, but only if you know that your listeners will be able to understand them. A short grab in simple language may be usable without an overdub, especially when it is used to show the emotion behind a speech, rather than the content.

It is occasionally possible to open the bulletin with dramatic piece of actuality, then explain it with a back-announcement.

Such a grab must be dramatic, short and make sense to your listeners.

For example, a radio journalist used a 10-second grab of guns firing and people screaming during the assassination of Egyptian President Anwar Sadat, then back-announced: "The guns which destroyed the hopes of peace in the Middle East as President Anwar Sadat of Egypt was assassinated."

Only use such opening grabs on special occasions, otherwise they lose their effect. Also, it is not good to play the grab before the opening theme, as it will confuse your listeners.

Music

Never use music as background to a news bulletin. It is distracting and ruins any variations in pace within the bulletin.

A special theme should be used to announce the bulletin and may occasionally be used within the bulletin, perhaps to separate different segments. We call such short music inserts stabs.

Your opening theme should be short and dramatic. Many record companies now produce selections of electronic or instrumental themes especially for use as stabs. Any stabs within the bulletin should echo the opening theme as a link throughout the bulletin. However, too many stabs will annoy the listener and reduce the amount of time available for real news.

It is possible to use a closing theme at the end of the bulletin, although this should be different from the opening theme (you do not want to fool your listeners into thinking that this is the start of the bulletin). The best compromise is to use the opening bars of a theme at the start of the bulletin and use the closing bars at the end.

Timing Your Bulletin

There is never enough time on radio for all the stories a journalist would like to include, so the timing of your bulletin is very important. By careful timing you will be able to include all your important stories, giving adequate details of each.

The exact time of each item depends upon:

- How long the whole bulletin is;
- How many items you need to include;
- How many grabs of actuality you want to use.

You have to balance these three considerations. If your bulletin is 15 minutes long you can use up to 20 stories, several of them with grabs, and still treat each story properly. If the bulletin is only five minutes, long you might not manage more than seven or eight items and have time for only one or two short pieces of actuality.

Because some important stories can be told briefly and some less important stories need lots of explanation, you cannot set a fixed time for each story. However, if you aim to tell each story in about 30 to 45 seconds, you will be able to cover the news properly and in some detail.

If you have a number of less important stories which you want to mention, run them as briefs at the end of the bulletin. Briefs are short stories, no longer than one or two sentences each. They are not designed to tell the whole news, simply to let people know that something has happened.

The inclusion of briefs also helps to increase the pace of the bulletin if the rest of the stories are long and heavy.

If you are a newsreader too, you must always read your bulletin through fully before going to air. Use this opportunity to time each item, writing the time in the bottom right-hand corner. Eventually you will be able to look at a piece of copy and estimate within a second how long it will take to read. Initially, timing each item with a watch will help you to develop the skill. Some modern newsroom computer systems can automatically calculate the duration of a story based on the number of words and the newsreader's reading rate.

Below, in the section Reading rate, we give some practical advice on how to calculate the length of your bulletin and its components. Always take more copy than you need into the studio, just in case you have misjudged your timing or you have problems with a piece of audio which does not play. The extra copy may be a story which you would not normally consider important enough for the bulletin, but which will provide a useful reserve in emergencies.

Keep glancing at the studio clock as you read the bulletin so that you can make adjustments, adding or taking away stories. And always be ready to use that extra story in an emergency. In some cases, when your bulletin comes before a current affairs segment, you will not need to run full details of some stories in the news. You can say something like: "We will have full details of this story in our current affairs program after this bulletin."

Special Bulletins

We have been speaking so far mainly about regular news bulletins. There are, however, special bulletins which need considering.

News Flashes

A news flash is when the newsreader breaks into a program on-air to read an important, urgent news story, such as a major disaster or the death of a national leader. The news flash should only be used on extremely important stories.

Urgent news which arrives in the studio as the bulletin is going to air should be read at the next most suitable break in the bulletin, although it usually makes sense to use it at the end of the bulletin, just before any closing headlines.

The newsreader should have the story as soon as possible, so that they can decide where in the bulletin to use it. If you intended ending the bulletin with a light story and the flash comes through of a major air crash, you must drop the light story.

It is possible to interrupt a non-news program for a news flash, although you must warn people in the studio that you are coming with the flash. The best method of introducing a flash is for the program presenter to introduce the newsreader with words like: "Now we interrupt the program to cross over to the newsdesk for some urgent news." The newsreader should then read the story in their usual tone, speaking clearly and repeating details. If you only have one sentence, you can read it twice to get the message across clearly. You should end with words like: "Those are all the details available at the moment. We will give full details in our next bulletin, at six o'clock."

Weekend Bulletins

You may need to treat weekend news bulletins in a slightly different way from weekday bulletins, because there are usually fewer stories available.

You will need to re-assess newsworthiness at weekends, perhaps running stories which you would not use at other times. Your listeners will understand this. In fact, they may even welcome a change from a diet of death, disaster and politics.

You may want to make your weekend bulletins shorter and perhaps include a segment on sports news. You may want to save lighter stories during the week to run at the weekend, as long as you still cover the major events as well.

Practical Techniques

There are many practical techniques which will make the job of preparing news bulletins easier and more professional. If you use these techniques, they will help you to overcome many of the problems which inexperienced journalists can encounter.

Ranking Stories

One of the major problems in bulletin preparation is ranking the stories in correct order. Just follow some simple steps.

First read through all the stories available. Then go through them again, making three lists (or selecting the stories on to three piles). These categories should be:

1. Important stories which you must use;
2. Stories which you can use, but which are not so important;

3. Stories which you cannot use, for any reason.

First look at the stories in category one. Calculate roughly how much news these will give you (if each story will be approximately 40 seconds long and you have four of them, they will take about 2 minutes 40 seconds to read).

Now choose enough stories from category two to more than fill the remaining time. Together with your essential category one stories, decide the order in which you want to use them, taking into account their importance, length and pace.

You can combine stories on similar topics, either running them as one story or as two stories linked with words such as "Meanwhile" or "Still on the subject of...". A word of caution. Do not combine too many stories, because they will become a shapeless mass and you will lose the impact of separate intros.

Reading Rate

It is very useful to know your reading rate or the reading rate of the newsreader who will read the bulletin. Once you know how long it will take you (or the newsreader) to read one line of type, you can time your bulletin by counting lines, rather than by timing yourself each time you practice.

Reading rates are calculated in words per second (wps) and usually range from 2 wps for slower readers in some languages to 3.5 wps for quite rapid readers in other languages. Ask a colleague to help you calculate your reading rate. Get them to time 60 seconds while you read a short piece of news script.

Mark where you stop after 60 seconds. Add up how many words you read in 60 seconds and write this number down. Repeat this process ten more times with different scripts. To calculate the average number of words you read in 60 seconds, add up all the numbers from the ten scripts and divide the total by ten. Divide this figure by 60 to get your reading rate in words per second.

For example, you might find that over 10 scripts, you read 125, 126, 119, 123, 118, 120, 122, 126, 118 and 117 words in 60 seconds. Add these up; they total 1214 words. Divide this by 10 to get the average number of words per script (121). Now divide this average by 60 to get the number of words per second. The answer is roughly 2 words per second-your average reading rate.

Once you know your average reading rate, you can estimate how long it will take to read each story. Of course, you will not want to count all the words in all your stories; this would take too long. It is better to count just the number of lines.

First, count how many words there are in 50 lines of your standard news scripts, then divide the total by 50. This will give you the average number of words per line. For example, if there are 600 words in 50 lines of script, the average is 12 words per line.

Now you can calculate how long it takes you to read a line of script. For example, if your reading rate is 2 words per second and your script contains an average of 12 words per line, you can read one line in 6 seconds (12 divided by 2). By counting the total number of lines in each story, you can calculate quite accurately how long they will take to read. For example, a story with 8 lines of type will take 48 seconds to read (8 times 6). Mark the time on the bottom right-hand corner of each story.

One final step is to add up the times for all your stories. This will tell you the total time it will take to read them all. When you are adding up total reading time for the bulletin, add an extra two seconds for the pause between each story.

(One tip on counting lines: If the final line in the paragraph ends less than half way across the page, ignore it. Count only those lines which end more than half way across the page. Over a number of paragraphs, this will average out accurately.)

Of course, you may need a calculator to work out all the sums, but it is worth the effort. Once you learn how to calculate the length of your bulletins, you will be able to time them accurately. After many years, you may become so experienced that you can judge the length of a bulletin just by looking at it.

The Script

Most newsrooms today use computers to produce news stories and features which newsreaders can either print out or read directly from a screen in the studio.

If your newsroom uses printed scripts they must be typed neatly, with any last-minute changes clearly crossed out. If you make more than a couple of crossings-out, re-print that script.

Start a new paragraph for each sentence and type double-spaced. Type only one story per sheet, as this will make it easier to find stories if you want to drop or insert them during the bulletin. Use good quality paper which will not rustle as you move it.

Never turn a phrase from one line to the next and certainly never hyphenate words from one line to the next.

Never staple the pages of your bulletin together. You must be able to pull the sheets aside noiselessly as you read them. Stack the stories neatly on one side after you have read them; do not throw them on the floor.

Even if you read "off the screen", much of the above advice still holds though the challenge now is how to manage the scrolling of the script and the re-arrangement of stories while you read. As mentioned earlier, television newsreaders usually read from an autocue operated by another member of the production staff. Radio newsreaders seldom have such help so have to present their bulletins single-handed.

Whether you work in radio and television, if your news stories and bulletins are well-prepared in an orderly manner, you will make your work easier and serve your audience more effectively.

To Summarise:

- KISS-keep it short and simple
- Do not use quotes on radio or in television scripts
- Avoid unfamiliar words
- Repeat important words

- Keep punctuation simple
- Simplify numbers
- Avoid abbreviations
- Show how to pronounce difficult words

When constructing bulletins consider:

- balance
- pace

Remember radio and television news is presented in a linear way over time.

Consider how you will use different elements and how they go together in sequence.

Time your bulletin precisely but always have extra material in reserve.

2

Audio Broadcasting

- 1916: First regular broadcasts on 9XM (now WHA)-Wisconsin state weather, delivered in Morse Code
- 1919: First clear transmission of human speech, (on 9XM) after experiments with voice (1918) and music (1917).
- 1920: Regular wireless broadcasts for entertainment began in Argentina, pioneered by the group around Enrique Telemaco Susini.
- 1920: Spark-gap telegraphy stopped.
- 20 August 1920: E.W. Scripps's WWJ in Detroit received its commercial broadcasting license and started broadcasting. It has carried a regular schedule of programming to the present. Broadcasting was not yet supported by advertising. The stations owned by manufacturers and department stores were established to sell radios and those owned by newspapers to sell papers and express the opinions of the owners.
- 31 August 1920: The first known radio news program was broadcast by station 8MK, the unlicensed predecessor of WWJ (AM) in Detroit, Michigan.
- October 1920: Westinghouse in Pittsburgh, Pennsylvania became the first US commercial broadcasting station to be licensed when it was granted call letters KDKA. (Their engineer Frank Conrad had been broadcasting from his own station since 1916.)

- 1922: Regular wireless broadcasts for entertainment began in the UK from the Marconi Research Centre at Writtle near Chelmsford, England. Early radios ran the entire power of the transmitter through a carbon microphone.
- Mid 1920s:
- Amplifying vacuum tubes revolutionized radio receivers and transmitters; Westinghouse engineers improved them. (Before that, the commonest type of receiver was the crystal set, although some early radios used some type of amplification through electric current or battery.)
  - o Inventions of the triode amplifier, generator, and detector enabled audio radio.
  - o Fessenden and Lee de Forest pioneered the invention of amplitude-modulated radio (AM radio), so more than one station can send signals (as opposed to spark-gap radio, where one transmitter covers the entire bandwidth of spectra). Westinghouse bought DeForest's and Armstrong's patent.
- 1920s: Radio was first used to transmit pictures visible as television.
- Early 1930s: Single sideband (SSB) and frequency modulation (FM) were invented by amateur radio operators. By 1940, they were established commercial modes.

Westinghouse was brought into the patent allies group, General Electric, American Telephone and Telegraph, and Radio Corporation of America, and became a part owner of RCA. All radios made by GE and Westinghouse were sold under the RCA label 60% GE and 40% Westinghouse.

ATT's Western Electric would build radio transmitters. The patent allies attempted to set up a monopoly, but they failed due to successful competition. Much to the dismay of the patent allies, several of the contracts for inventor's patents held clauses protecting "amateurs" and allowing them to use the patents. Whether the competing manufacturers were really amateurs was ignored by these competitors.

These features arose:-

- Commercial (United States) or governmental (Europe) station networks
- Federal Radio Commission
- Federal Communications Commission
- Birth of the soap opera
- Race towards shorter waves and FM
- 1933: FM radio was patented; Edwin H. Armstrong invented it. FM uses frequency modulation of the radio wave to minimize static and interference from electrical equipment and the atmosphere, in the audio program.
- 1937: W1XOJ, the first experimental FM radio station, was granted a construction permit by the FCC.
- 1940s: Standard analog television transmissions started in North America and Europe.
- 1943: Tesla's patent (number *645576*) was reinstated by the U.S. Supreme Court shortly after Tesla's death, because prior art existed before Marconi's patent was established. Ignoring Tesla's prior art, the decision may have let the U.S. government avoid paying damages that the Marconi Company was claiming for use of its patents during World War I; it is speculated that the U.S. government initially refused to grant Marconi the patent right, to nullify any claims Tesla had for compensation.
- After World War II: The FM radio broadcast was introduced in Germany.
- 1948: A new wavelength plan was set up for Europe at a meeting in Copenhagen. Because of the recent war, Germany (which was not even invited) was only given a few medium-wave frequencies, which are not very good for broadcasting. For this reason Germany began broadcasting on USW, "ultra short wave" (nowadays

called VHF). After some amplitude modulation experience with VHF, it was realized that FM radio was a much better alternative for VHF radio than AM.

Later 20th Century Developments

- Early 1960s: VOR systems finally became widespread; before that, aircraft used commercial AM radio stations for navigation. (AM stations are still marked on U.S. aviation charts).
- 1954: Regency introduced a pocket transistor radio, the TR-1, powered by a "standard 22.5V Battery".
- 1960: Sony introduced their first transistorized radio, small enough to fit in a vest pocket, and able to be powered by a small battery. It was durable, because there were no tubes to burn out. Over the next twenty years, transistors displaced tubes almost completely except for very high power, or very high frequency, uses.
- 1963: Colour television was commercially transmitted, and the first (radio) communication satellite, Telstar, was launched. In late 1960s, the U.S. long-distance telephone network began to convert to a digital network, employing digital radios for many of its links.
- 1970s: LORAN became the premier radio navigation system. Soon, the U.S. Navy experimented with satellite navigation.
- 1987: The GPS constellation of satellites was launched.
- Early 1990s: Amateur radio experimenters began to use personal computers with audio cards to process radio signals.
- 1994: The U.S. Army and DARPA launched an aggressive successful project to construct a software radio that could become a different radio on the fly by changing software.
- Late 1990s: The digital transmissions began to be applied to broadcasting.

Telex on Radio

Telegraphy did not go away on radio. Instead, the degree of automation increased. On land-lines in the 1930s, Teletypewriters automated encoding, and were adapted to pulse-code dialing to automate routing, a service called telex. For thirty years, telex was the absolute cheapest form of long-distance communication, because up to 25 telex channels could occupy the same bandwidth as one voice channel. For business and government, it was an advantage that telex directly produced written documents.

Telex systems were adapted to short-wave radio by sending tones over single sideband. CCITT R.44 (the most advanced pure-telex standard) incorporated character-level error detection and retransmission as well as automated encoding and routing. For many years, telex-on-radio (TOR) was the only reliable way to reach some third-world countries. TOR remains reliable, though less-expensive forms of e-mail are displacing it. Many national telecom companies historically ran nearly pure telex networks for their governments, and they ran many of these links over short wave radio.

21st Century Development

Internet Radio

When Internet-based radio became feasible in the mid-1990s, the new medium required no licensing and stations could broadcast from anywhere in the world without the need for over the air transmitters. This greatly reduced the overhead for establishing a station, and in 1996, George Maat started 'A' Net Station (A.N.E.T.) under the now defunct domain Advice-Net.com, and began broadcasting commercial-free from Antarctica.

MIT developed the "Radio Locator" List of Radio Stations. After stations started streaming audio on the Internet, Radio-Locator added this to their search engine so anyone could locate a station's website and listen to a station offering a worldwide stream. This list also tracks "terrestrial" radio stations who may not have live audio on the net, or even a website, but are able to find station information by various other search queries.

Types

Transmission and Reception Schematic

The best known type of radiostation are the ones that broadcast via radiowaves. These include foremost AM and FM stations. There are several subtypes, namely commercial, public and nonprofit varieties as well as student-run campus radio stations and hospital radio stations can be found throughout the developed world.

Although now being eclipsed by internet-distributed radio, there are many stations that broadcast on shortwave bands using AM technology that can be received over thousands of miles (especially at night). For example, the BBC has a full schedule transmitted via shortwave. These broadcasts are very sensitive to atmospheric conditions and solar activity.

Also, many other non-broadcast types of radio stations exist. These include base stations for police, fire and ambulance networks, military base stations, dispatch base stations for taxis, trucks, and couriers, emergency broadcast systems, and amateur radio stations.

Arbitron, the United States based company which reports on radio audiences defines a “radio station” as one of: government-licensed AM or FM station an HD Radio (primary or multicast) station, an internet stream of an existing government-licensed station or one of the satellite radio channels from XM Satellite Radio or Sirius Satellite Radio.

Over Radiowaves

AM Broadcasting

“AM Radio” redirects here. For the song by Everclear, see AM Radio (song).

AM broadcasting is the process of radio broadcasting using amplitude modulation.

History

AM was the dominant method of broadcasting during the first eighty years of the 20th century and remains widely used into the 21st.

AM radio began with the first, experimental broadcast on Christmas Eve of 1906 by Canadian experimenter Reginald Fessenden, and was used for small-scale voice and music broadcasts up until World War I. San Francisco, California radio station KCBS claims to be the direct descendant of KQW, founded by radio experimenter Charles "Doc" Herrold, who made regular weekly broadcasts in San Jose, California as early as June of 1909. On that basis KCBS has claimed to be the world's oldest broadcast station and celebrated its 100th anniversary in the summer of 2009.

The great increase in the use of AM radio came late in the following decade as radio experimentation increased worldwide following World War I. The first licensed commercial radio services began on AM in the 1920s. XWA of Montreal, Quebec (later CFCF, now CINW) claims status as the first commercial broadcaster in the world, with regular broadcasts commencing on May 20, 1920. The first licensed American radio station was started by Frank Conrad, KDKA in Pittsburgh, Pennsylvania. Radio programming boomed during the "Golden Age of Radio" (1920s–1950s). Dramas, comedy and all other forms of entertainment were produced, as well as broadcasts of news and music.

Operation

AM radio technology is simpler than FM radio, DAB, Satellite Radio and HD Radio. An AM receiver detects amplitude variations in the radio waves at a particular frequency. It then amplifies changes in the signal voltage to drive a loudspeaker or earphones. The earliest crystal radio receivers used a crystal diode detector with no amplification.

In North American broadcasting practice, transmitter power input to the antenna for commercial AM stations ranges from about 250 watts to 50,000 watts. Experimental licenses were issued for up to 500,000 watts radiated power, for stations intended for wide-area communication during disasters including Cincinnati station WLW, which used such power on occasion before World War II. WLW's superpower transmitter still exists at the station's suburban transmitter site, but it was decommissioned in the early 1940s and no current commercial broadcaster in the US or Canada is authorized for such power levels. Some other countries do authorize higher power operation (for example the Mexican station XERF formerly operated at 250,000 watts). Antenna design must consider the coverage desired and must direct the transmitted signal so as not to interfere with other stations operating on the same or adjacent frequencies.

An example of the differance in range of an am radio at different times.

Medium-wave and short-wave radio signals act differently during daytime and nighttime. During the day, AM signals travel by groundwave, diffracting around the curve of the earth over a distance up to a few hundred miles (or kilometers) from the signal transmitter. However, after sunset, changes in the ionosphere cause AM signals to travel by skywave, enabling AM radio stations to be heard much farther from their point of origin than is normal during the day.

This phenomenon can be easily observed by scanning an AM radio dial at night. As a result, many broadcast stations are required as a condition of license to reduce their broadcasting power significantly (or use directional antennas) after sunset, or even to suspend broadcasting entirely during nighttime hours. In the United States and Canada, some AM radio stations are granted clear channel status, meaning that they broadcast on frequencies with few other stations allocated, allowing an extended coverage area. Relatively few stations enjoy clear-channel status. Commercial broadcasters generally rely on the ground-wave coverage only as their target market for advertising.

The hobby of listening to long distance signals is known as DX or DX'ing, from an old telegraph abbreviation for "distance". Several non-profit hobbyist clubs are devoted exclusively to DXing the AM broadcast band, including the National Radio Club and International Radio Club of America. Similarly, people listening to short wave transmissions are SWLing.

Frequency Bands

AM radio is broadcast on several frequency bands. The allocation of these bands is governed by the ITU's Radio Regulations and, on the national level, by each country's telecommunications administration (the FCC in the U.S., for example) subject to international agreements.

- *Long wave* is 148.5 kHz–283.5 kHz, with 9 kHz channel spacing generally used. Long wave is used for radio broadcasting in Europe, Africa and parts of Asia (ITU region 1), and is not allocated in the Western Hemisphere. In the United States and Canada, Bermuda and U.S. territories this band is mainly reserved for aeronautics navigational aids, though a small section of the band could theoretically be used for microbroadcasting under the United States Part 15 rules. Due to the propagation characteristics of long wave signals, the frequencies are used most effectively in latitudes north of 50°.
- *Medium wave* is 520 kHz–1,610 kHz. In the Americas (ITU region 2) 10 kHz spacing is used; elsewhere it is 9 kHz. ITU region 2 also authorizes the Extended AM broadcast band between 1610 kHz and 1710 kHz. Medium wave is by far the most heavily used band for commercial broadcasting. This is the "AM radio" that most people are familiar with.
- *Short wave* is 1.711 MHz–30.0 MHz, divided into 15 broadcast bands. Shortwave broadcasts generally use a narrow 5 kHz channel spacing. Short wave is used by audio services intended to be heard at great distances from the transmitting station. The long range of short wave broadcasts comes at the expense of lower audio fidelity. The mode of propagation for short wave is

different. AM is used mostly by broadcast services – other shortwave users may use a modified version of AM such as SSB or an AM-compatible version of SSB such as SSB with carrier reinserted.

Frequencies between the broadcast bands are used for other forms of radio communication, and are not broadcast services intended for reception by the general public.

Limitations

Because of its susceptibility to atmospheric and electrical interference, AM broadcasting now attracts mainly talk radio and news programming, while music radio and public radio mostly shifted to FM broadcasting in the late 1970s. However, in the late 1960s and 1970s, top 40 rock and roll stations in the US and Canada such as WABC and CHUM transmitted highly processed and extended audio to 11 kHz, successfully attracting huge audiences. In the UK during the 1980s, BBC Radio 4 (a largely speech channel) had an FM location, whereas BBC Radio 1, a music channel, was confined to AM broadcasts over much of the UK. Frequency response is typically 40 Hz–5 kHz with a 50 dB S/N ratio.

The limitation on AM fidelity comes from current receiver design. Moreover, to fit more transmitters on the AM broadcast band, in the United States maximum transmitted audio bandwidth is limited to 10.2 kHz by an NRSC standard adopted by the FCC in June of 1989, resulting in a channel occupied bandwidth of 20.4 kHz. The former audio limitation was 15 kHz resulting in a channel occupied bandwidth of 30 kHz.

AM radio signals can be severely disrupted in large urban centres by metal structures, tall buildings and sources of radio frequency interference (RFI) and electrical noise, such as electrical motors, fluorescent lights, or lightning.

As a result, AM radio in many countries has lost its dominance as a music broadcasting service, and in many cities is now relegated to news, sports, religious and talk radio stations. Some musical genres – particularly country, oldies, nostalgia and ethnic/world music– survive on AM, especially in areas where FM frequencies are in short supply or in thinly populated or mountainous areas where FM coverage is poor.

Other Distribution Methods

Stereo transmissions are possible, and hybrid digital broadcast systems are now being used around the world. In the United States, Biquity's proprietary HD Radio has been adopted and approved by the FCC for medium wave transmissions, while Digital Radio Mondiale is a more open effort often used on the shortwave bands, and can be used alongside many AM broadcasts. Both of these standards are capable of broadcasting audio of significantly greater fidelity than that of standard AM with current bandwidth limitations, and a theoretical frequency response of 0-16 kHz, in addition to stereo sound and text data. While FM radio can also be received by cable, AM radio generally cannot, although an AM station can be converted into an FM cable signal. In Canada, cable operators that offer FM cable services are required by the CRTC to distribute all locally available AM stations in this manner. In Switzerland a system known as "wire broadcasting" transmits AM signals over telephone lines in the longwave band.

Microbroadcasting

Some microbroadcasters and pirate radio broadcasters, especially those in the United States under the FCC's Part 15 rules, broadcast on AM to achieve greater range than is possible on the FM band. On mediumwave (AM), such radio stations are often found between 1610 kHz and 1710 kHz. Hobbyists also use low-power AM transmitters to provide local programming for antique radio equipment in areas where AM programming is not widely available or is of questionable quality; in such cases the transmitter, which is designed to cover only the immediate property and perhaps nearby areas, is hooked up to a computer or music player.

FM Broadcasting

FM broadcasting is a broadcast technology invented by Edwin Howard Armstrong that uses frequency modulation (FM) to provide high-fidelity sound over broadcast radio.

Terminology

The term 'FM band' is effectively shorthand for 'frequency band in which FM is used for broadcasting'. It can upset purists because it conflates a modulation scheme with a range of frequencies.

The term 'VHF' (Very High Frequency) was previously in common use in Europe. 'UKW', which stands for *Ultrakurzwellen* (ultra short wave) in German is still widely used in Germany, as is 'UKV' (*Ultrakortvåg*) in Sweden.

Broadcast Bands

Throughout the world, the broadcast band falls within the VHF part of the radio spectrum. Usually 87.5 to 108.0 MHz is used, or some portion thereof, with few exceptions:

- In the former Soviet republics, and some former Eastern Bloc countries, the older 65-74 MHz band is also used. Assigned frequencies are at intervals of 30 kHz. This band, sometimes referred to as the OIRT band, is slowly being phased out in many countries. In those countries the 87.5-108.0 MHz band is referred to as the CCIR band.
- In Japan, the band 76-90 MHz is used.

The frequency of an FM broadcast station (more strictly its assigned nominal centre frequency) is usually an exact multiple of 100 kHz. In most of the Americas and the Caribbean, only odd multiples are used. In some parts of Europe, Greenland and Africa, only even multiples are used. In Italy, multiples of 50 kHz are used. There are other unusual and obsolete standards in some countries, including 0.001, 0.01, 0.03, 0.074, 0.5, and 0.3 MHz.

Modulation Characteristics

Pre-Emphasis and De-Emphasis

Random noise has a 'triangular' spectral distribution in an FM system, with the effect that noise occurs predominantly at the highest frequencies within the baseband. This can be offset, to a limited extent, by boosting the high frequencies before transmission and reducing them by a corresponding amount in the receiver. Reducing the high frequencies in the receiver also reduces the high-frequency noise. These processes of boosting and then reducing certain frequencies are known as pre-emphasis and de-emphasis, respectively.

The amount of pre-emphasis and de-emphasis used is defined by the time constant of a simple RC filter circuit. In most of the world a 50 μs time constant is used. In North America, 75 μs is used. This applies to both mono and stereo transmissions and to baseband audio (not the subcarriers). The amount of pre-emphasis that can be applied is limited by the fact that many forms of contemporary music contain more high-frequency energy than the musical styles which prevailed at the birth of FM broadcasting. They cannot be pre-emphasized as much because it would cause excessive deviation of the FM carrier. (Systems more modern than FM broadcasting tend to use either programme-dependent variable pre-emphasis—e.g. dbx in the BTSC TV sound system—or none at all.)

FM Stereo

In the late 1950s, several systems to add stereo to FM radio were considered by the FCC. Included were systems from 14 proponents including Crosley, Halstead, Electrical and Musical Industries, Ltd. (EMI), Zenith Electronics Corporation and General Electric. The individual systems were evaluated for their strengths and weaknesses during field tests in Uniontown, Pennsylvania using KDKA-FM in Pittsburgh as the originating station. The Crosley system was rejected by the FCC because it degraded the signal-to-noise ratio of the main channel and did not perform well under multipath RF conditions.

In addition it did not allow for SCA services because of its wide FM sub-carrier bandwidth. The Halstead system was rejected due to lack of high frequency stereo separation and reduction in the main channel signal-to-noise ratio. The GE and Zenith systems, so similar that they were considered theoretically identical, were formally approved by the FCC in April 1961 as the standard stereo FM broadcasting method in the USA and later adopted by most other countries. It is important that stereo broadcasts should be compatible with mono receivers.

For this reason, the left (L) and right (R) channels are algebraically encoded into sum (L+R) and difference (L"R) signals. A mono receiver will use just the L+R signal so the listener will hear both channels in the single loudspeaker. A stereo receiver will add the L+R and L"R signals to recover the Left channel, and subtract the L+R and L"R signals to recover the Right channel. For example, if in a certain moment in time, a station wishes to broadcast the following signals, L=5 and R=3, then L+R=8 whereas L-R=2. The station will broadcast these two signals, 8 and 2. The receiver will now recreate the original signals like this: L=(8+2)/2=5, R=(8-2)/2=3.

The (L+R) Main channel signal is transmitted as baseband audio in the range of 30 Hz to 15 kHz. The (L"R) Sub-channel signal is modulated onto a 38 kHz double-sideband suppressed carrier (DSBSC) signal occupying the baseband range of 23 to 53 kHz.

A 19 kHz pilot tone, at exactly half the 38 kHz sub-carrier frequency and with a precisely defined phase relationship to it, is also generated. This is transmitted at 8–10% of overall modulation level and used by the receiver to regenerate the 38 kHz sub-carrier with the correct phase.

The final multiplex signal from the stereo generator contains the Main Channel (L+R), the pilot tone, and the sub-channel (L"R). This composite signal, along with any other sub-carriers (SCA), modulates the FM transmitter. Converting the multiplex signal back into left and right audio signals is performed by a stereo decoder, which is built into stereo receivers.

In order to preserve stereo separation and signal-to-noise parameters, it is normal practice to apply pre-emphasis to the left and right channels before encoding, and to apply de-emphasis at the receiver after decoding.

Stereo FM signals are more susceptible to noise and multipath distortion than are mono FM signals. This is due to imbalance of FM sideband ratios of the additional modulating signals created by the pilot tone and the sub-carrier channel.

In addition, for a given RF level at the receiver, the signal-to-noise ratio for the stereo signal will be worse than for the mono receiver. The point at which the receiver input RF level reaches maximum monaural signal-to-noise ratio will be 23 dB lower than the receiver input RF level for maximum stereo signal-to-noise ratio.

For this reason many FM stereo receivers include a stereo/mono switch to allow listening in mono when reception conditions are less than ideal, and most car radios are arranged to reduce the separation as the signal-to-noise ratio worsens, eventually going to mono while still indicating a stereo signal is being received.

Quadraphonic FM

In 1969 Louis Dorren invented the Quadraplex system of single station, discrete, compatible four-channel FM broadcasting. There are two additional subcarriers in the Quadraplex system, supplementing the single one used in standard stereo FM. The baseband layout is as follows:

- 50 Hz to 15 kHz Main Channel (sum of all 4 channels) (LF+LB+RF+RB) signal, for mono FM listening compatibility.
- 23 to 53 kHz (cosine quadrature subcarrier) (LF+LB)-(RF+RB) Left minus Right difference signal. This signal's modulation in algebraic sum and difference with the Main channel was used for 2 channel stereo listener compatibility.
- 23 to 53 kHz (sine quadrature 38 kHz subcarrier) (LF+RF)-(LB+RB) Front minus Back difference signal. This signal's modulation in algebraic sum and difference with the Main channel and all the other subcarriers is used for the Quadraphonic listener.
- 61 to 91 kHz (cosine quadrature 76 kHz subcarrier) (LF+RB)-(LB+RF) Diagonal difference signal. This signal's modulation in algebraic sum and difference

with the main channel and all the other subcarriers is also used for the Quadraphonic listener.

- 95 kHz SCA subcarrier, phase-locked to 19 kHz pilot, for reading services for the blind, background music, etc.

There were several variations on this system submitted by GE, Zenith, RCA, and Denon for testing and consideration during the National Quadraphonic Radio Committee field trials for the FCC. The original Dorren Quadraplex System outperformed all the others and was chosen as the national standard for Quadraphonic FM broadcasting in the United States. The first commercial FM station to broadcast quadraphonic program content was WIQB (now called WWWW-FM) in Ann Arbor/Saline, Michigan under the guidance of Chief Engineer Brian Brown.

Other Subcarrier Services

Typical spectrum of composite baseband signal (25 kHz lower bound should read 23 kHz)

The subcarrier system has been further extended to add other services. Initially these were private analog audio channels which could be used internally or rented out. Radio reading services for the blind are also still common, and there were experiments with quadraphonic sound. If stereo is not on a station, everything from 23 kHz on up can be used for other services. The guard band around 19 kHz (±4 kHz) must still be maintained, so as not to trigger stereo decoders on receivers. If there is stereo, there will typically be a guard band between the upper limit of the DSBSC stereo signal (53 kHz) and the lower limit of any other subcarrier.

Digital services are now also available. A 57 kHz subcarrier (phase locked to the third harmonic of the stereo pilot tone) is used to carry a low-bandwidth digital Radio Data System signal, providing extra features such as Alternative Frequency (AF) and Network (NN). This narrowband signal runs at only 1187.5 bits per second, thus is only suitable for text. A few proprietary systems are used for private communications. A variant of RDS is the North American RBDS or "smart radio" system. In Germany the analog ARI system was used prior to RDS for broadcasting traffic announcements to motorists (without disturbing other listeners). Plans to use ARI for other European countries led to the development of RDS as a more powerful system. RDS is designed to be capable of being used alongside ARI despite using identical subcarrier frequencies.

In the United States, digital radio services are being deployed within the FM band rather than using Eureka 147 or the Japanese standard ISDB. This in-band on-channel approach, as do all digital radio techniques, makes use of advanced compressed audio. The proprietary Biquity system, branded as "HD Radio", currently is authorized for "hybrid" mode operation, wherein both the conventional analog FM carrier and digital sideband subcarriers are transmitted. Eventually, presuming widespread deployment of HD Radio receivers, the analog services could theoretically be discontinued and the FM band become all digital.

In the USA services (other than stereo, quad and RDS) using subcarriers are sometimes referred to as SCA (subsidiary communications authorisation) services. Uses for such subcarriers include book/newspaper reading services for blind listeners, private data transmission services (for example sending stock market information to stockbrokers or stolen credit card number blacklists to stores) subscription commercial-free background music services for shops, paging ("beeper") services and providing a program feed for AM transmitters of AM/FM stations. SCA subcarriers are typically 67 kHz and 92 kHz.

Dolby FM

A commercially unsuccessful noise reduction system used with FM radio in some countries during the late 1970s, Dolby FM used a modified 25 μs pre-emphasis time constant and a frequency selective companding arrangement to reduce noise.

Distance Covered by an FM Stereo Transmission

The range of an FM mono transmission is related to the

transmitter RF power, the antenna gain and antenna height. The FCC (USA) publishes curves that aid in calculation of this maximum distance as a function of signal strength at the receiving location. For FM stereo, the maximum distance covered is significantly reduced. This is due to the presence of the 38 kHz subcarrier modulation. Vigorous audio processing improves the coverage area of an FM stereo station.

Adoption of FM Broadcasting Worldwide

Despite having been patented in 1933, commercial FM broadcasting was not authorized until January 1, 1941. It took many years for FM to be adopted by the majority of radio listeners.

The first FM broadcasting stations were in the United States, but initially they were primarily used to broadcast classical music to an upmarket listenership in urban areas and for educational programming. By the late 1960s FM had been adopted by fans of "Rock Music" ("A.O.R.-'Album Oriented Rock' Format"), but it wasn't until 1978 that listenership to FM stations exceeded that of AM stations. During the 1980s and 1990s, Top 40 music stations and later even country music stations largely abandoned AM for FM. Today AM is mainly the preserve of talk radio, news, sports, religious programming, ethnic (minority language) broadcasting and some types of minority interest music. Ironically, this shift has transformed AM into the "alternative band" that FM once was. Belgium, the Netherlands, Denmark and particularly West Germany were among the first countries to adopt FM on a widespread scale. Among the reasons for this were:

1. The medium wave band in Western Europe is heavily overcrowded, leading to severe interference problems and, as a result, most MW frequencies are suitable only for speech broadcasting.
2. Particularly in Germany after World War II, the best available medium wave frequencies were used by the Allied occupation forces both for broadcasting entertainment to their troops and for broadcasting cold war propaganda across the Iron curtain.

3. The regional structure of German broadcasting meant that the few remaining AM frequencies available for civilian domestic broadcasting fell far short of the number required and the broadcasters looked to FM as an alternative.

Public service broadcasters in Ireland and Australia were far slower at adopting FM radio than those in either North America or continental Europe. However, in Ireland several unlicenced commercial FM stations were on air by the mid-1980s. These generally simulcast on AM and FM.

In the United Kingdom, the BBC began FM broadcasting in 1955, with three national networks carrying the Light Programme, Third Programme and Home Service (renamed Radio 2, Radio 3 and Radio 4 respectively in 1967). These three networks used the sub-band 88.0 – 94.6 MHz. The sub-band 94.6 to 97.6 MHz was later used for BBC and local commercial services. Only when commercial broadcasting was introduced to the UK in 1973 did the use of FM pick up in Britain. With the gradual clearance of other users (notably Public Services such as police, fire and ambulance) and the extension of the FM band to 108.0 MHz between 1980 and 1995, FM expanded rapidly throughout the British Isles and effectively took over from LW and MW as the delivery platform of choice for fixed and portable domestic and vehicle-based receivers.

In addition, Ofcom (previously the Radio Authority) in the UK issues on demand Restricted Service Licences on FM and also on AM (MW) for short-term local-coverage broadcasting which is open to anyone who does not carry a prohibition and can put up the appropriate licensing and royalty fees. In 2006 almost 500 such licenses were issued.

FM started in Australia in 1947 but did not catch on and was shut down in 1961 to expand the television band. It was not reopened until 1975. Subsequently, it developed steadily until in the 1980s many AM stations transferred to FM because of its superior sound quality. Today, as elsewhere in the developed world, most Australian broadcasting is on FM – although AM talk stations are still very popular.

Most other countries expanded their use of FM through the 1990s. Because it takes a large number of FM transmitting stations to cover a geographically large country, particularly where there are terrain difficulties, FM is more suited to local broadcasting than national networks. In such countries, particularly where there are economic or infrastructural problems, "rolling out" a national FM broadcast network to reach the majority of the population can be a slow and expensive process.

ITU Conferences about FM

The frequencies available for FM were decided by some important conferences of ITU. The milestone of those conferences is the Stockholm agreement of 1961 among 38 countries.

- Final acts of the conference: A 1984 conference in Geneva made some modifications to the original Stockholm agreement particularly in the frequency range above 100 MHz.

Small-Scale Use of the FM Broadcast Band

Consumer Use of FM Transmitters

In some countries, small-scale (Part 15 in United States terms) transmitters are available that can transmit a signal from an audio device (usually an MP3 player or similar) to a standard FM radio receiver; such devices range from small units built to carry audio to a car radio with no audio-in capability (often formerly provided by special adapters for audio cassette decks, which are becoming less common on car radio designs) up to full-sized, near-professional-grade broadcasting systems that can be used to transmit audio throughout a property. Most such units transmit in full stereo, though some models designed for beginner hobbyists may not. Similar transmitters are often included in satellite radio receivers and some toys.

Legality of these devices varies by country. The FCC in the US and Industry Canada allow them. Starting on 1 Oct 2006 these devices became legal in most countries in the European

Union. Devices made to the harmonised European specification became legal in the UK on 8 Dec 2006.

FM Radio Microphones

The FM broadcast band can also be used by some inexpensive wireless microphones, but professional-grade wireless microphones generally use bands in the UHF region so they can run on dedicated equipment without broadcast interference. Such inexpensive wireless microphones are generally sold as toys for karaoke or similar purposes, allowing the user to use an FM radio as an output rather than a dedicated amplifier and speaker.

Microbroadcasting

Low-power transmitters such as those mentioned above are also sometimes used for neighborhood or campus radio stations, though campus radio stations are often run over carrier current. This is generally considered a form of microbroadcasting. As a general rule, enforcement towards low-power FM stations is stricter than AM stations due to issues such as the capture effect, and as a result, FM microbroadcasters generally do not reach as far as their AM competitors.

Clandestine use of FM Transmitters

FM transmitters have been used to construct miniature wireless microphones for espionage and surveillance purposes (covert listening devices or so-called "bugs"); the advantage to using the FM broadcast band for such operations is that the receiving equipment would not be considered particularly suspect. Common practice is to tune the bug's transmitter off the ends of the broadcast band, into what in the United States would be TV channel 6 (<87.9 MHz) or aviation navigation frequencies (>107.9); most FM radios with analog tuners have sufficient overcoverage to pick up these slightly-beyond-outermost frequencies, although many digitally tuned radios do not. Constructing a "bug" is a common early project for electronics hobbyists, and project kits to do so are available from a wide variety of sources. The devices constructed, however, are often too large and poorly shielded for use in clandestine activity. In addition, much pirate radio activity is broadcast in the FM range, because of the band's greater clarity and listenership, and the lower size and cost of equipment.

Campus Radio

Campus radio (also known as college radio, university radio or student radio) is a type of radio station that is run by the students of a college, university or other educational institution. Programming may be exclusively by students, or may include programmers from the wider community in which the station is based. Sometimes campus stations are operated for the purpose of training professional radio personnel, sometimes with the aim of broadcasting educational programming, while other stations exist to provide an alternative to commercial or government broadcasters.

Campus radio stations are generally licensed and regulated by national governments, and so have very different characteristics from one country to the next. One commonality between many stations regardless of their physical location is a willingness — or, in some countries, even a licensing requirement — to broadcast musical selections that are not categorized as commercial hits. Because of this, campus radio has come to be associated with emerging musical trends, including genres such as punk and New Wave, alternative rock, India rock and hip hop, long before those genres become part of the musical mainstream. Campus radio stations also often provide airplay and promotional exposure to new and emerging local artists.

Many campus radio stations carry a variety of programming including news (often local), sports (often relating to the campus), and spoken word programming as well as general music. Often the format is best described as a freeform radio format, with a lot of creativity and individualism among the disc jockeys and show hosts. A number of these stations have gained critical acclaim for their programming and are considered by the community in which they are embedded to be an essential media outlet.

Although the term *campus radio* implies full-power AM or FM transmission over the air, many stations experiment with low-power broadcasting, closed circuit or carrier current systems, often to on-campus listeners only. Some stations are distributed through the cable television network on cable FM or the second audio program of a TV station. Some universities and colleges broadcast one or more Internet radio feeds — either instead of, or in addition to a campus radio station — which may differ in format significantly from licensed traditional campus radio.

Campus Radio around the World

Belgium

- *Radio Campus* (University Libre de Bruxelles).

Canada

In Canada, radio stations are regulated by the Canadian Radio-television and Telecommunications Commission (CRTC) which provides that "a campus radio station is a station owned or controlled by a not-for-profit organization associated with a post-secondary educational institution". The CRTC distinguishes two types of campus radio: *instructional* (for training of professional broadcasters) and *community-based campus* (programming provided by volunteers who are not training to be professionals). The community-based format is the predominant one, colloquially known as "campus-community radio." In recent years, some community-based campus radio stations, including CFFF-FM in Peterborough and CJMQ-FM in Sherbrooke, have in fact had their CRTC licenses formally reclassified from campus radio to community radio.

Campus radio stations broadcasting at full power are assigned a permanent frequency and call letters and, aside from a requirement not to compete directly with commercial stations, are full players in the Canadian broadcasting spectrum. Campus radio stations in Canada are more commonly associated with universities than with colleges, although some colleges also have licensed campus radio stations. As well, some institutions maintain unlicensed campus radio operations which broadcast only by closed circuit, cable FM or Internet streaming. The first licensed community-based campus radio station was CKCU-FM, based at Carleton University in Ottawa, which first broadcast on November 14, 1975. Prior to this date, some developmental university radio projects had previously produced and aired programs on commercial radio stations, and CJRT-FM, a campus radio station of the instructional type, had been on air since 1949. CFRC at Queen's University in Kingston has been on the air since 1923; however, until the 1940s it was a commercial radio station and even a Canadian Broadcasting Corporation affiliate. Unlike most campus radio stations, however, CFRC was owned for much of its history by the university itself, rather than by the student government.

The CRTC places responsibilities upon campus radio stations in Canada through the use of *conditions of license* that stations must follow in order to keep broadcasting. Campus stations, for example, are expected to be leaders in the Canadian content system which mandates a minimum number of Canadian musical selections throughout the day. In early 2005, Humber College's radio station CKHC-FM became the first broadcast station in Canada to air 100% Canadian content. Other requirements generally made of campus stations include quotas of non-hit, folk and ethnic musical selections as well as spoken word programming.

Most campus radio stations in Canada are members of the National Campus and Community Radio Association.

France

IASTAR (International Association of Student Television And Radio) is the French student radios association.

The IASTAR radio stations include:

- Ajaccio : Radio Voce Studentina 103.2
- Amiens : Radio Campus Amiens 88.7
- Angers : Radio Campus Angers 103.0
- Bastia : Radio Voce Studentina 98.9
- Besançon : Radio Campus Besançon 102.4

- Bordeaux : Radio Campus Bordeaux 88.1
- Brest : Radio-U 101.1
- Caen : Radio Phoenix 92.7
- Clermont-Ferrand : Radio Campus Clermont-Ferrand 93.3
- Corte : Radio Voce Studentina 104.0
- Dijon : Radio Dijon Campus 92.2
- Grenoble : Radio Campus Grenoble 90.8
- Lille : Radio Campus Lille 106.6
- Lyon : Radio Brume 90.7
- Marseille : Radio Grenouille 88.8
- Orleans : Radio Campus Orleans 88.3
- Paris : Radio Campus Paris 93.9
- Rennes : Radio Campus Rennes 88.4
- Strasbourg : Radio En Construction 90.7
- Toulouse : Radio Campus Toulouse 94.0
- Tours : Radio Campus Tours 99.5

India

Community groups in India, and non-governmental organisations (NGOs) have been campaigning for permission to set up *community radio* (CR) stations since the late nineties. But the government, particularly under the earlier Bharatiya Janata Party (BJP), allowed the setting up of campus radio stations by educational institutions.

News, as of November 2006, has it that the India cabinet decided to grant permission to non-profit organizations and educational institutions to set up community radio stations. The cabinet decision will allow civil society and voluntary organizations, state agriculture universities and institutions, Krishi Vigyan Kendras or agricultural science centres, registered societies and autonomous boards and public trusts registered under Societies Act to start community radio stations. Ravi Shankar Prasad, the then Minister for Information and

Broadcasting in the BJP-lead National Democratic Alliance government, told India's upper house of parliament the Rajya Sabha on December 22, 2003, that four organizations including Jammu University and Kashmir University were found ineligible for grant of license as per the laid down guidelines. The minister also ruled out any review of the policy despite limited response to the non-commercial, low-powered FM radio scheme which former information and broadcasting minister Sushma Swaraj had said would "revolutionize" radio broadcast in the country.

Radio enthusiast Alokesh Gupta saying: "The announcement of the Government was to have seen 1000 radio stations by December 2003. Instead administrative wrangling came in the way of implementing the project as colleges spent time running around for licenses and approval from four ministries — Home Affairs, Communications & Information & Broadcasting — as they took their time processing applications."

On February 2, 2004, Anna University in Chennai unveiled the country's first campus radio station, Anna FM. Radio Ujjas in Kutch (in the western state of Gujarat) is one such CR and gets its funding from the United Nations Development Programme (UNDP) and the Central Government. Similarly a community .based radio programme titled Panchayat Vani (People's Voice) was recently broadcast on All India Radio (AIR), Darbhanga, Bihar. The campus station Gyanvaani has also been licensed.

Pune University is the first university in the state of Maharashtra to have an FM station. The University of Pune's FM Radio inaugurated on May 1, 2005, has been named as Vidyavani. It covers a wide range of subjects, focusing specifically on the requirements of students of various departments and affiliated colleges. It reaches an area around the campus within eight-km radius.

Unsuccessful attempts have been also made to start CR without obtaining any permission. The small village of Orvakal in Kurnool district of Andhra Pradesh (South India) launched "Mana Radio" (Our Radio) in November 2002. This project run under the aegis of the Society for Elimination of Rural Poverty used a tiny transmitter that covered a radius of half a kilometer to enable rural women members of self help groups. Four months later, officials from the Central Government brought in police to seize the equipment and declared the broadcasts illegal.

The Government policy to permit educational institutions to have their own FM Channels at low frequency levels emerged in mid December 2002, as a result of years of campaigning by activists and a strongly-worded Supreme Court judgment directing the opening up of the airwaves.

A unique experiment in using media technologies, especially radio, for development and empowerment of marginalized, rural communities is the community radio initiative "Chalo Ho Gaon Mein" a programme that is broadcast once a week on AIR Daltonganj in the Palamu district of Jharkhand, eastern India. This radio programme is supported by the National Foundation for India and produced by Community representatives, of Alternative for India Development (AID), a non-governmental organization.

According to the terms of the campus broad license, a number of aspects are disallowed from broadcasts. This includes anything that offends good taste or decency, contains criticism of friendly countries, contains an attack on religion, contains anything obscene, defamatory, false and suggestive innuendos and half truths, likely to encourage or incite violence, contains anything affecting the integrity of the nation, criticizes, maligns or slanders any individual in person, encourages superstition or blind belief, denigrates women, denigrates children, or presents or depicts or suggests as desirable the misuse of drugs, alcohol, narcotics, and tobacco.

Israel

Campus radio also exists in Israel, where several colleges, universities and high schools have successful programs. One of the most famous is Kol HaCampus (Voice of the Campus/ Campus Voice), broadcast out of Tel Aviv on 106 MHz. More information can be found with the Israeli Broadcasting

Authority. Another college radio station is the HebrewItaly University's in Jerusalem, broadcasting mostly India and alternative music.

Italy

Radio Bocconi Università Commerciale Luigi Bocconi di Milano.

Pakistan

- *radio.lums.edu.pk RadioLUMS-Gal Sunn Oye* (Lahore University of Management Sciences)
- *Karachi university campus radio FM 90.6* (University of Karachi).

Poland

- *Students Radio ¯ak* (Technical University of Lodz)
- *Akademickie Radio LUZ* (Wroclaw University of Technology).

Portugal

In Portugal, there are several college and university radio stations continuously broadcasting programs. *Radio Universidade de Coimbra* and *Radio Universidade Morae*, founded in 1986, are the oldest university student radio stations in the country still in operation. There are also many online-only radio sites belonging to higher education institutions.

Portugal's major college and university radio stations include:

- *Radio Universidade de Coimbra* (University of Coimbra)
- *Radio Universidade Morae* (Tras-os-Montes and Alto-Douro University)
- *Radio Universidade da Beira Interior* (University of Beira Interior)
- *Radio Universidade do Algarve* (University of the Algarve)
- *Radio Universidade do Minho* (Minho University)
- *Radio Zero* (Instituto Superior Tecnico).

Switzerland

Frequency Banane is the student radio in Lausanne on EPFL and UNIL campus. It exists since 1993 and is broadcasting on the Internet and CATV network on FM 94.55 MHz in Lausanne and region. In the past Frequency Banane has broadcast with former Radio Acidule from 1992 to 1996 and then had its independent FM transmitter operating on 92.4 MHz from 1998 to 2005. In 2005, Swiss frequency regulation authority (BAKOM) decided to end the low power FM licence. Radio Radius is an uprising campus radio in Zurich on ETHZ and UNIZH campus. It's broadcasting on the Internet only. Radius is trying to get a permanent licence to broadcast on FM but it is very hard in Zurich. Right now Radius is negotiating with BAKOM.

United Kingdom

In the United Kingdom, campus radio is generally referred to as Student Radio. University of Hertfordshire's Crush Radio was the first student radio founded in 1960 followed by University Radio York, founded in 1967, and Swansea University's station Action Radio (today called Xtreme Radio) in 1968.

Some student radio stations operate on the FM waveband for short periods at a time under the Restricted Service Licence scheme, while others choose to broadcast full-time on the AM waveband using an LPAM licence. There are only five UK student radio stations permitted to broadcast all year on LPFM. These are Xpression FM (Exeter), Radio Roseland (Truro, Cornwall), Storm FM (Bangor), Bailrigg FM (Lancaster) and 1386 HCR (Halesowen College). None of these licences provides for a reception area greater than four kilometres from the point of transmission. To counteract these licence restrictions and, in the case of AM broadcasts, poor quality audio, many stations simulcast on the Internet.

The UK Student Radio Association works on behalf of more than fifty UK-based member stations to further their development, encourage and facilitate communication between member stations and links to the commercial radio industry, and lobby for the membership's interests on both a regional and national level. The association organises and hosts the annual Student Radio Awards in conjunction with BBC Radio 1.

United States

College radio (as it is generally known in the United States) became commonplace in the 1960s when the Federal Communications Commission (FCC) began issuing class D licenses for ten watt stations to further the development of the then new FM band. Some colleges had already been broadcasting for decades on the AM band, often originating in physics experiments in the early 20th century. One of the first college radio stations in the country is WRUC from Union College in Schenectady, New York. Its first experimental broadcasts under the call sign 2ADD were in 1920. Most of the FM stations received higher-class licenses than ten watts, typically a few hundred watts. A few got several kilowatts, and a small handful got licenses in the range of tens of thousands, sometimes reaching up to maximum-power 100-kilowatt outlets. Still, due to strict class D regulations, some stations were prohibited from a wattage upgrade for possible signal interference with adjacent stations, such as KWUR 90.3 FM interfering with KWMU 90.7 FM in St. Louis, Missouri.

The earliest college radio stations carried news, intercollegiate sports, and music along with educational shows and sometimes distance learning courses. In the latter portion of the 20th century, many U.S. stations played what came to be known as "college rock" (later known as alternative rock), a type of rock music that had not yet hit the mainstream. Most stations have now diversified, with many following a very commercial-like music rotation during the weekdays, and having specialty shows on evenings and weekends. A few stations really go out on a limb, occasionally being described as a cacophony of randomness.

College stations are typically considered to be public radio stations in they way that they are funded by donation and grants, but as a radio format the term "public radio" generally refers to classical music, jazz, and news. A more accurate term is community radio, as most staff are volunteers, although many stations limit staff to current or recent students instead cf anyone from the local community.

By the late 1970s, FM had taken off, and competition for channels for new stations was intensifying. The National Association of Broadcasters (NAB) and the newly-founded National Public Radio (NPR) convinced the FCC that local low-power stations were somehow detrimental to broadcasting, and class D licenses were no longer issued for applications made after 1979, except for broadcast translators to repeat NAB and NPR members' stations. Making matters worse, the stations were demoted to a second-class status, meaning that they would be forced off the air if any full-power station wanted their space.

Many stations were forced to upgrade their facilities at considerable expense to the students. Many other stations were eventually (and still continue to be) forced off the air, because they could not afford the upgrades at all, or not in time to avoid being locked-in by other expanding stations.

There have also been situations where some college radio stations have been forced off the air by a school administration. In one instance, the student media director of WUSC-FM in Columbia, South Carolina implied that the station's broadcast license had been "flagged" by the FCC due to an out of control staff and inappropriate songs being played on public airwaves. This serious charge proved to be false, but it led directly to WUSC, which had been named as 1992 *Spin* College Radio Station of the Year, being shut down in 1995.

The entire executive board of the station (students elected by their peers) was fired for supposedly promoting a culture of irresponsibility. This caused most student DJs to quit in protest. After silence for 45 days, WUSC came back-but it had abandoned its popular alternative music format, playing songs it never allowed before. As a result, *College Music Journal* and the now-defunct *Gavin Report* dropped WUSC as a reporter of new music they played on air.

Many college stations in the U.S. also carry syndicated programming, such as that of National Public Radio and affiliated regional networks. Some stations have had their student programming forced off the air and taken for other uses, such as WWGC and KTXT. The original WGST was the subject of an involuntary takeover which saw the state's board of regents sell the station out from under Georgia Tech as "surplus" property.

A very few stations have been added to the airwaves in very isolated cities with the return of the LPFM license to the U.S. The restrictions that the U.S. Congress placed on LPFM stations as a result of the NAB's misleading lobbying have seriously limited the effectiveness of this, however. HD Radio also also creates RF interference which LPFM stations cannot object to, and which they cannot convert to themselves because it is cost-prohibitive even for many commercial radio stations. A number of college stations have been shut out of traditional broadcasting methods and are available only as streaming audio over the Internet. Some stations use a variety of methods, such as Michigan State University's WDBM ("The Impact") and Northern Kentucky University's WNKU. Both stations broadcast traditionally, as well as in HD, and via online streaming.

Sweden

- Radio AF in Lund
- Radio AFB
- Studentradion 98,9 in Uppsala
- K103 in Gothenburg
- Pite FM in Pitea
- Radio Campus in Orebro.

Norway

- Radio Nova, Oslo
- Studentradioen i Bergen, Bergen
- Studentradion i Trondheim, Trondheim.

Guatemala

- Radio Universidad.

Hospital radio

Hospital radio is a form of audio broadcasting produced specifically for the in-patients of hospitals. It is primarily found in the United Kingdom.

History

The earliest known hospital radio station officially commenced operation in the Walter Reed General Hospital, Washington, D.C., in May 1919.

The first in the United Kingdom was installed at York County Hospital, England, in 1925. Headphones were provided beside 200 beds, and 70 loudspeakers were installed, with patients being able to listen to sports commentaries and church services. Throughout the 1930s radio stations spread to a handful of other hospitals, with live music supplementing the speech-based programmes. Unsurprisingly, virtually no new stations were started during World War II, the sole exception being on Jersey where a service was set up to relay church services, musical recitals, variety shows, and programmes for children to nine hospitals after wireless receivers had been banned and confiscated by the German occupying authorities.

The spread of hospital radio services picked up slowly in the late 1940s. The 1950s saw a rapid growth in their number in the UK, with similar stations opening in the Netherlands, Japan, and the United States. Many stations now played gramophone music to patients and, with the launch of the cassette tape in 1963, it became easy for presenters to record their programmes for playback at a later date.

Hospital radio stations peaked in number in the 1980s, when up to 300 stations are thought to have been broadcasting on a daily basis. However as small hospitals closed or merged to form large regional medical centres, hospital radio stations also consolidated into a smaller number of larger organisations. New studios were built, often to a very high specification, and in common with commercial radio, hospital stations began to use CDs to play music.

Transmission

In the past, hospital radio tended to be delivered to patients' bedsides by way of a dedicated cable link from the in-house studio to a unit beside every bed. In some cases, this unit would have supplied only the hospital radio station; in others, a choice of broadcast radio stations may also have been available. Today, many stations are carried at a higher quality on the bedside entertainment systems of third party companies such as Hospedia (formerly Patientline). Others are broadcast from a central radio transmitter, by virtue of a low-powered AM or FM licence. Many hospital radio stations also broadcast over the Internet.

Organisation

Each hospital radio station was founded independently and they are not centrally organised or managed. Almost all are members of the Hospital Broadcasting Association (HBA), which was set up by stations for their mutual benefit and does not govern or run them. Most in the UK are registered charities, others are part of larger organisations such as hospital Leagues of Friends.

Hospital radio stations are staffed and managed by volunteers (more than 2,500 in the UK alone), and each volunteer is commonly attached to a particular weekly programme. Some broadcast, others work to keep the station's record library or computer systems up-to-date, but most also visit the hospital wards, to discuss the music that patients would like to hear, and to provide an opportunity for the latter to converse with a member of non-medical staff.

Many stations use sophisticated computerised playout systems for music and jingles. Live programming is limited to the times that stations' volunteer members can attend studios-generally evenings and weekends-but many stations offer a 24-hour service by using computerised systems to play music and prerecorded programmes at other times.

There are more than 230 hospital radio stations in the UK, and 170 in the Netherlands. Others operate in Germany, France, Norway, Australia, United States and New Zealand.

Many professional radio presenters volunteer for hospital radio in their early career, as it provides a training ground for budding broadcasters. Such broadcasters include:

- Andrew Edwards, now of BBC Radio Leeds, was previously with Kingstown Radio, the Hospital Radio service in Kingston upon Hull.
- Daniel Fox, now of Heart Northants, was previously with Hospital Radio Ipswich.
- Paul Moseley, now of BBC Radio Norfolk was previously with Hinchingbrooke Hospital Radio in Huntingdon.
- James Dundon, now of Pirate FM was previously with Royal Cornwall Hospital radio.

Emergency Broadcast System

The Emergency Broadcast System (EBS) was an emergency warning system in the United States, used from 1963 to 1997, when it was replaced by the Emergency Alert System.

Purpose

"The Emergency Broadcast System was established to provide the President of the United States with an expeditious method of communicating with the American public in the event of war, threat of war, or grave national crisis." It replaced CONELRAD on August 5, 1963. In later years, it was expanded for use during peacetime emergencies at the state and local levels.

Although the system was never used for a national emergency, it was activated more than 20,000 times between 1976 and 1996 to broadcast civil emergency messages and warnings of severe weather hazards. Some dramatic works depicting nuclear warfare (most notably the 1983 made-for-TV film *The Day After*) included fictionalized scenes of EBS activations.

National Level EBS

An order to activate the EBS at the national level would have originated with the President and been relayed via the White House Communications Agency duty officer to one of two origination points: either the Aerospace Defense Command or the Federal Preparedness Agency—as the system stood in 1978. Participating telecommunications common carriers, radio and television networks, the Associated Press and United Press International would receive and authenticate (by means of code words) an Emergency Action Notification via an EAN teletypewriter network designed specifically for this purpose. These recipients would relay the EAN to their subscribers and affiliates.

The release of the EAN by the ADC or FPA would initiate a process by which the common carriers would link otherwise independent networks such as ABC, CBS and NBC into a single national network that even independent stations could receive programming from.

"Broadcast stations would have used the two-tone Attention Signal on their assigned broadcast frequency to alert other broadcast stations to stand by for a message from the President." Note that the transmission of programming on a broadcast station's assigned frequency, and the fact that television networks/stations could participate, distinguished EBS from CONELRAD. EBS radio stations would not transmit on 640 or 1240 AM, and television stations would carry the same audio program as AM radio stations..

Activation Procedure

Actual activations originated with a primary station, which would transmit the Attention Signal. The Attention Signal most commonly associated with the EBS was a combination of the sine waves of 853 and 960 Hz, a completely disharmonic combination that is extremely offensive to the human ear, and hence, perfectly suited to getting the audience's collective attention. Decoders at relay stations would sound an alarm, alerting the station operator to the incoming message. Then each relay station would broadcast the alert tone and rebroadcast the emergency message from the primary station. The sine wave combination for the EBS signal was seen on the EBS slide from WXYZ-TV in Detroit, Michigan from the late 70s to 1992.

A nationwide activation of the EBS was called an Emergency Action Notification (EAN). This was the only type of activation which broadcast stations were not allowed to ignore; the FCC made local civil emergencies and weather advisories optional (except for stations that had agreed to be the "primary" source of such messages).

To activate the EAN protocol, the AP and UPI wire services would notify stations with a special message. It began with a full line of X's, and a bell inside the teletype machine would sound ten times. To avoid abuse and mistakes, the message included a confirmation password which changed daily. Stations that subscribed to one of the wire services were not required to activate the EBS if the activation message did not have proper confirmation.

False Alarm of 1971

Despite these safeguards, the system was inadvertently activated at 9:33 AM EST on February 20, 1971. Teletype operator W. S. Eberhardt accidentally "played the wrong tape" during a test of the system. As a result, an EBS activation message authenticated with the codeword "hatefulness" was sent through the entire system, ordering stations to cease regular programming and broadcast the alert of a national emergency. A cancellation message was sent at 9:59 AM EST; however, it used the same codeword again. A cancellation message with the correct codeword, "impish," was not sent until 10:13 AM EST.

This false alarm demonstrated major flaws in the EBS system. Many stations had not received the alert, but more importantly, the vast majority of those that did ignored it, or did not know what to do during an emergency. The only station in the country that shut down as mandated by FCC rules was WSNS-TV (Ch 44) in Chicago. Numerous investigations were launched, and several changes were made to the EBS. Among them, the on-air alert announcement was streamlined, eliminating language that warned the audience of an imminent attack against the country.

"If This Had Been an Actual Emergency..."

Although it was never used, the FCC's EBS plan involved detailed procedures for stations to follow during an EAN. It included precise scripts that announcers were to read at the outset of the emergency and whenever detailed information was scarce.

Among other things, citizens were instructed not to use the telephone, but rather continue listening to broadcast stations for information. As official information began to emerge from various sources, non-primary stations were to broadcast it according to the following priority list:

- Messages from the president
- Statewide emergency information
- Local emergency information (for a station's operational area, i.e. evacuation and sheltering plans)
- National programming and news (other than a presidential message).

A presidential message was always required to be aired live during an EAN. For other information, stations were to follow the priority list to decide what should be disseminated first. Lower priority official programming was to be recorded for the earliest available rebroadcast.

Participation in EAN emergency broadcasting was done with the "voluntary cooperation" of each station (as noted in the classic test announcement). Stations that were not prepared to be part of the national EBS network were classified as "non-participating" by the FCC. During an EAN, a non-participating station was required to advise listeners/viewers to tune elsewhere to find emergency bulletins. The station's transmitter would then be turned off. Non-participating stations had to remain off-the-air until the EAN was terminated. Under no circumstances could any broadcast station continue with normal programming during a national emergency.

Testing the System

Until the system was superseded, radio and television stations were required to perform a *Weekly Transmission Test Of The Attention Signal and Test Script* on random days and times between 8:30 A.M and local sunset. Stations were required to perform the test at least once a week and were only exempt from performing the test if they had activated the EBS for a state or local emergency or participated in a coordinated state or local EBS test during the past week.

Additionally, stations were required to log tests they received from each station they monitored for EBS messages. This served as an additional check, as they could expect to hear a weekly test from each source. Failure to receive a signal at least once a week meant that either the monitored station was having a problem transmitting the alert signal, or the monitoring station was having a problem receiving it.

Original Plan

Early in the history of the EBS, tests and activations were initiated in a similar way to CONELRAD tests. Primary stations would turn their transmitters off for five seconds, back on for five seconds, off for five seconds more, then would go back on air and transmit a 1000 Hz tone for 15 seconds to alert secondary stations. This quick off-and-on became known to broadcast engineers as the "EBS Stress Test", as older transmitters would sometimes fail after the quick cycling on and off. This became unnecessary as broadcast technology advanced and the two-tone alarm was developed.

Later Test Pattern

Later on, the EBS Stress Test was scrapped in favour of the following procedure:

1) Normal programming was suspended. Television stations would transmit a video slide such as the one illustrating this entry (numerous designs were available over the years). One of the following announcements written below was transmitted:

- *"This is a test. For the next sixty* (or thirty) *seconds, this station will conduct a test of the Emergency Broadcast System. This is only a test."*
- "(name of host station in a particular market) *is conducting a test of the Emergency Broadcast System. This is only a test."* (Mainly radio stations used this particular announcement)
- *"This is a test. This station is conducting a test of the Emergency Broadcast System. This is only a test."*
- *"The following is a test of the Emergency Broadcast System."*

2) The Attention Signal was transmitted from the EBS encoder for 20 to 25 seconds. At the special request of the FCC, however, this step was occasionally (though rarely) skipped.
3) The announcement written below (depending on the variation) was transmitted. The first part read:

- *"This is a test of the Emergency Broadcast System. The broadcasters of your area in voluntary cooperation with the FCC and other authorities* (or, in later years, "federal, state and local authorities") *have developed this system to keep you informed in the event of an emergency."*

There were a number of variations for the second half of the statement. During the early days of the system, stations other than the designated primary station for an operational area were required to shut down in the event of an emergency (reminiscent of the CONELRAD days), and the message was a variation of:

- *"If this had been an actual emergency, you would have been instructed to tune to one of the broadcast stations in your area."*
- *"If this had been an actual emergency, you would have been instructed where to tune in your area for news and official information".*

By the early 1980s, as it became easier for stations to record and relay messages from a primary station, and the risk of hostile bombers using broadcast signals to navigate lessened due to the development of ICBMs, the requirement to shut down in the event of activation was dropped, and the message became:

- *"If this had been an actual emergency, the Attention Signal you just heard would have been followed by official information, news or instructions."*

As the EBS was about to be replaced by its successor, the aforementioned Emergency Alert System, some stations used the following variant:

- *"This station is testing its Emergency Broadcast System equipment. The EBS will soon be replaced by the Emergency Alert System; the EAS will provide timely emergency warnings."*

The test concluded with one of the following phrases:

- "(sponsoring station in a particular market) *serves the* (name of operational area) *area. This concludes this test of the Emergency Broadcast System."*
- *"This station serves the* (name of operational area) *area. This concludes this test of the Emergency Broadcast System."*

These variations were heard in different parts of the country throughout the years depending on FCC regulations at the time, local preferences, and whether the specific station performing the test was a primary EBS station or not.

At least one version made explicit reference to an attack on the United States as being a possible scenario for EBS activation. The announcement text was mandated by the FCC.

Stations had the option of either reading the test script live, or using recorded versions. Jingle producer Terry Moss (of "L.A. Air Force" fame) offered a sung version of the most common script on his *Cheap Radio Thrills* and WHEN radio in Syracuse, New York had their own sung version. In the late 1970s, however, the FCC prohibited singing the test script or reading it as if it were a joke.

Purpose of the Test and Cultural Impact

The purpose of the test was to allow the FCC and broadcasters to verify that EBS tone transmitters and decoders were functioning properly. In addition to the weekly test, test activations of the entire system were conducted periodically for many years. These tests showed that about 80% of broadcast outlets nationwide would carry emergency programming within a period of five minutes when the system was activated.

The weekly broadcast of the EBS test message made it part of American cultural fabric of the era, and became the subject of all kinds of jokes and skits. Comedian Jon Stewart made fun of the EBS in a 1996 Miami stand-up performance; he called it a "useless piece of shit," saying, "What if you're not watching TV or listening to the radio? Do they come to your door?" He then slapped his palm against his microphone to imitate door knocks, and then screamed, "Aaaaaaaaaaaaaaaah!" Several people have testified about being frightened by the Test Pattern and attention signal as children, and actual emergencies scared them even more.

Comedian Adele Givens did a bit questioning why the EBS wasn't used to warn the American public on 9/11, talking about how she expected to hear the voice-over guy (whom she referred to as "Ted") delivering news about the attacks.

The band Negativland used the WHEN/Syracuse jingle version of the EBS script in their live performance "It's All In Your Head FM".

Prong used an EBS test message in the song "Test" on their 1994 album, Cleansing.

Amateur Radio Station

An amateur radio station is an installation designed to provide radiocommunications in the amateur radio service for an amateur radio operator. Radio amateurs build and operate several types of amateur radio stations, including fixed ground stations, mobile stations, space stations, and temporary field stations. A slang term often used for an amateur station's location is the shack, named after the small enclosures added to the upperworks of naval ships to hold early radio equipment and batteries.

Types of Stations

Fixed Stations

An amateur radio station established in a permanent structure with equipment that is not intended for portable operation is referred to as a *fixed station*. This is the most common form of amateur radio station, and can be found in homes, schools, and some public buildings. A typical fixed station is equipped with a transceiver and one or more antennas. For voice communications, the station will be equipped with a microphone; for communications using the Morse code, a telegraph key is common; and for communications over digital modes such as RTTY and PSK31, a station will be equipped with a specialized interface to connect the transceiver to a computer sound card. While not a requirement for radiocommunications, most fixed amateur radio stations are equipped with one or more computers, which serve tasks ranging from logging of contacts with other stations to various levels of station hardware control. Fixed stations might also be equipped with amplifiers, antenna rotators, SWR meters, and other station accessories.

Fixed stations are generally powered from the AC mains electrical supply available in the building. Some equipment in fixed stations may run off low voltage DC instead of AC, and require a separate power supply. Some fixed stations are equipped with auxiliary sources of power, such as electrical generators or batteries for use in emergencies.

Mobile Stations

An amateur radio station installed in a vehicle is referred to as a *mobile station*. A typical mobile station is equipped with a transceiver, one or more antennas, and a microphone. The transceiver may be specially designed for installation in vehicles. It may be much smaller than transceivers designed for fixed station use, to facilitate installation under a seat or in a trunk, and it may feature a detachable control head that can be mounted in a separate location from the rest of the radio. Antennas designed for mobile stations must accommodate the unique physical constraints of the vehicle and travel lanes which it occupies, allowing for clearance under overpasses and bridges, and safe passage by vehicles in adjacent lanes.

Most antennas used in mobile stations are omnidirectional. Few mobile stations are equipped to communicate with Morse code or digital modes. Most mobile stations are designed to be operated by the vehicle operator while driving. Most transceivers installed in vehicles are designed to run on 12-16 VDC, and are generally powered by the starting battery in the vehicle. Because of the power demands placed on the vehicle battery, most mobile stations either do not include external amplifiers or include amplifiers with power outputs that are more modest than those commonly found in fixed stations.

A specialized form of mobile station used for competition in a VHF amateur radio contest in North America is called a *rover station*. A rover station is often designed to be operated by a passenger in the vehicle rather than the driver, and may include multiple transceivers, transverters, directional antennas, and a laptop computer to log contacts made.

While it may not be a regulatory requirement, many mobile stations will append a*/M* to end of their call sign (pronounced as "slash mobile" on phone) while operating to identify themselves to other stations as a mobile station. Rover station operating in a VHF contest will append a*/R* to the end of their call sign (pronounced "slash rover").

Maritime mobile stations are mobile stations installed in a watercraft, usually an ocean-going vessel. When in international waters, these stations are operated under the regulatory authority of the flag under which the vessel is registered. In addition to the regulatory requirements of amateur radio, operation of maritime mobile stations also requires the permission of the captain of the vessel. Maritime mobile stations append a*/MM* to end of their call sign (pronounced as "slash maritime mobile").

Aeronautical mobile stations are mobile stations installed in an aircraft. In addition to the regulatory requirements of amateur radio, operation of aeronautical mobile stations also requires the permission of the pilot of the aircraft. Aeronautical mobile stations append a/*AM* to end of their call sign (pronounced as "slash aeronautical mobile").

Portable Stations

An amateur radio station set up in a temporary location is referred to as a *portable station*. A portable stations might be established to provide emergency communications in a disaster area, to provide public service communications during a large organized event such as a charity bicycle ride, to provide communications during an expedition, or for the recreational enjoyment of operating outdoors. Portable stations include the same basic equipment as fixed and mobile stations, although transportation of the transceiver, antennas, power supplies or batteries and necessary accessories often influences the particular selection. Equipment that does not weigh very much, or that can be broken down for shipment or transportation in luggage is especially popular with amateur radio operators travelling on DX-Peditions.

Most portable stations rely upon generator or battery power. Because this form of power might be of limited supply, portable stations often operate at lower transmitter power output to conserve energy.

Some portable stations append a/*P* to end of their call sign (pronounced as "slash portable") to indicate their status as a portable operation. In some countries, this is a regulatory requirement, whereas in others it is done at the option of the operator.

Space Stations

An amateur radio station that is located in a satellite, the Space Shuttle, or on the International Space Station is referred to as a *space station*. Some countries, including the United States, have additional or different regulations regarding the operation of space stations than other amateur radio stations.

Most space stations are located on satellites that orbit the earth. These stations are frequently either transponders or repeaters that operate under automatic control and can be used by *ground stations* (any station that is not a space station) to relay their signal to other ground stations.

Handheld Stations

Handheld radios contain all the necessary equipment for radiocommunications with another station. A typical radio used as a *handheld station* integrates a transceiver with an antenna and a battery in one handheld package. Most handheld transceivers used in amateur radio are designed for operation on the VHF or UHF amateur radio bands and most often are capable of only FM voice communications transmissions. To conserve battery power, they have limited transmitter power, often below 1W, to cover a local range of typically a few km or miles.

Repeater Stations

An amateur radio repeater is a specialty amateur radio station that extends the range of communications for other stations. A repeater uses a receiver tuned to one radio frequency and a transmitter tuned to another radio frequency. Other stations using a repeater station transmit on one frequency but listen for signals on the other frequency. If a repeater station is in a favourable location, such as on a tall tower, the top of a tall building, or on a mountaintop, stations that otherwise would not be able to communicate with each other can each use the repeater and establish two-way communications.

Repeater stations generally operate under automatic control. The control equipment is responsible for transmitting the repeater station's call sign at regular intervals. This identification is often done in Morse code. Some US repeater stations append a/*R* to end of their call sign or not (used to be required in the 80s and early 90s but no longer). Some may still have a vanity "WR#xxx" repeater license where #=0 thru 9 and xxx is any 3 letter combo but these callsigns are going away when they expire.

Amateur Radio License

An amateur radio license is a legal document or permit giving official permission to the license holder to operate an amateur radio station. The license typically permits the bearer to transmit a signal on designated radio frequencies in order to conduct two-way communications with other licensed stations. In some countries, an amateur radio license is necessary in order to purchase or possess amateur radio equipment. Amateur radio licenses are issued by governmental authorities, typically the ministry or office of telecommunications of a national government. An amateur radio license is only valid in the country in which it is issued, or in another country that has a reciprocal licensing agreement with the issuing country.

Both the requirements for and privileges granted to a licensee vary from country to country, but generally follow the international regulations and standards established by the International Telecommunications Union and World Radio Conferences. Most governments issue several different classes of license, usually structured to grant additional privileges to those who demonstrate additional knowledge and proficiency.

An individual granted an amateur radio license is referred to as an amateur radio operator. In most countries, an individual will be assigned a call sign with their license. In some countries, a separate "station license" is required for any station used by an amateur radio operator. Amateur radio licenses may also be granted to organizations or clubs. Some countries only allow ham radio operators to operate club stations. Others, such as Syria restrict all operation by foreigners to club stations only. Radio transmission permits are closely controlled by nations' governments because clandestine uses of radio can be made and because, in the HF portion of the radio spectrum, HF radio waves propagate beyond national boundaries by the laws of physics, making radio an international matter.

Licensing Requirements

Requirements for issuance of an amateur radio license vary from country to country and can include passing a test of radiocommunication and electronics theory, and various age, citizenship, and other background requirements. In most countries, prospective amateur radio operators are required to pass an examination that tests knowledge and understanding of the key concepts of electronics, radio equipment, antennas, radio propagation, RF safety, and the radio regulations of the government granting the license.

These examinations are sets of questions typically posed in either a short answer or multiple-choice format, with a passing grade determined by the percentage of questions answered correctly. Depending on the radio regulations of the government in question, examinations can be administered by bureaucrats, non-paid certified examiners, or previously licensed amateur radio operators. The ease with which an individual can acquire an amateur radio license varies from country to country.

In some countries, examinations may be offered only once or twice a year in the national capital, and can be inordinately bureaucratic (for example in India) or challenging because some amateurs must undergo difficult security approval (as in Iran). A handful of countries, currently only Yemen and North Korea, simply do not issue amateur radio licenses to their citizens, although in both cases a limited number of foreign visitors have been permitted to obtain amateur licenses in the past decade. Some developing countries, especially those in Africa, Asia, and Latin America, require the payment of annual license fees that can be prohibitively expensive for most of their citizens.

A few small countries may not have a national licensing process and may instead require prospective amateur radio operators to take the licensing examinations of a foreign country. In countries with the largest numbers of amateur radio licensees, such as Japan, the United States, Canada, and most of the countries in Europe, there are frequent license examinations opportunities in major cities.

In most large countries, several classes of amateur radio license are available. Typically, one class of license is intended for novices or beginners, another is intended for those with intermediate knowledge and skill, and one is reserved for those who have demonstrated a high level of knowledge and radiocommunications skill. An introductory license class (such as the "Technician Class" license in the United States, the "Basic Class" license in Canada, Grade II Restricted in India, or the "Foundation Class" license in the United Kingdom) will typically require the successful completion of a written or multiple choice examination, without any Morse code proficiency examination. Higher license classes generally require the completion of more demanding examinations, and may require that the person being tested demonstrate a basic level of proficiency in Morse code reception.

The "First Class" license in Japan requires the ability to receive and copy Morse code sent at a rate of 25 words per minute. This is faster than the Indian Advanced Grade which requires a proficiency of 12 wpm, American "Amateur Extra" Class, which required 20 WPM from inception in 1950 until the "restructuring" in 2000, at which time it dropped to 5 WPM. Morse Code requirements in the U.S. ended February 23, 2007, when new regulations took effect.

The granting of a separate license to a club or organization generally requires that an individual with a current and valid amateur radio license, who is in good standing with the telecommunications authority, assumes responsibility for any operations conducted under the club license of club call sign. A few countries may issue special licenses to novices or beginners that do not assign the individual a call sign, but require the newly-licensed individual to operate from stations licensed to a club or organization for a period of time before a higher class of license can be acquired.

Licensing Privileges

An amateur radio license grants its bearer many privileges in the use of radio frequency spectrum not available to those without a license. The bearer of an amateur radio license may transmit and conduct two-way communications on "bands" of radio frequencies that are either designated for the exclusive use of licensed amateur radio operators or where amateur radio operations are permitted to share the spectrum with other licensed services (such as short wave broadcasters, military stations, or land mobile services). Depending on the license class, an operator or station licensed in one country is generally allowed to communicate directly with similarly licensed amateur radio operators and stations in other countries.

In most countries, an amateur radio license issued to an individual assigns a call sign to that individual. An amateur radio operator uses a call sign on the air to legally identify the operator or station during any and all radiocommunication. In some countries, the call sign assigned to the station must always be used, whereas in other countries, the call sign of either the operator or the station may be used.

In most countries, an amateur radio license grants permission to the license holder to own, modify, and operate equipment that is not certified by a governmental regulatory agency. This encourages amateur radio operators to experiment with home-constructed or modified equipment. The use of such equipment must still satisfy national and international standards on spurious emissions.

The amount of output power and amateur radio licensee may legally use varies from country to country. For example, the highest license classes are permitted: 2 kilowatts in most countries of the former Yugoslavia, 1.5 kilowatts in the United States, 1 kilowatt in Belgium and Switzerland, 750 watts in Germany, 500 watts in Italy, 400 watts in India, Singapore & United Kingdom, and 150 watts in Oman. Lower license classes are often restricted to lower power limits. For example, the foundation license class in the United Kingdom has a limit of just 10 watts.

Reciprocal Licensing

A reciprocal licensing agreement between two countries allows the bearer of an amateur radio license in one country to legally operate an amateur radio station in the other country without having to obtain an amateur radio license from the country being visited, or the bearer of a valid license in one country can receive a separate license and a call sign in another country, both of which have a mutually-agreed reciprocal licensing approvals. Reciprocal licensing requirements vary from country to country. Some countries have bilateral or multilateral reciprocal operating agreements allowing hams to operate within their borders with a single set of requirements. Some countries lack reciprocal licensing systems.

History

In the countries where personal use of the radio spectrum was permitted at all, amateur radio licenses were generally not required until the 1930s. In the United States, amateur radio licenses have been required since 1912.

Amateur Radio Operator

An amateur radio operator is an individual who typically uses equipment at an amateur radio station to engage in two-way personal communications with other similar individuals on radio frequencies assigned to the amateur radio service. Amateur radio operators have been granted an amateur radio license by a governmental regulatory authority. As a component of their license, Amateur radio operators are assigned a call sign that they use to identify themselves during communication. There are about three million amateur radio operators worldwide.

Amateur radio operators are also known as radio amateurs or hams. The term 'ham' as a nickname for amateur radio operators originated in a pejorative usage by operators in commercial and professional radio communities. The word was subsequently welcomed by amateur radio operators, and it stuck. An amateur radio operator who has died is referred to by other amateur radio operators as a silent key.

Demographics

Few governments maintain detailed demographic statistics of their amateur radio operator populations, aside from recording the total number of licensed operators. The majority of amateur radio operators worldwide reside in Japan, the United States, Thailand, South Korea, and the nations of Europe. Only the governments of Yemen and North Korea currently prohibit their citizens from becoming amateur radio operators. In some countries, acquiring an amateur radio license is difficult because of the bureaucratic processes or fees that place access to a license out of reach for most citizens. Most nations permit foreign nationals to earn an amateur radio license, but very few amateur radio operators are licensed in multiple countries.

Gender

In the vast majority of countries, the population of amateur radio operators are predominantly male. In the United States, approximately 15% of amateur radio operators are women. In China, 12% of amateur radio operators are women. The Young Ladies Radio League is an international organization of female amateur radio operators.

A male amateur radio operator can be referred to as an OM, an abbreviation used in Morse code telegraphy for "old man", regardless of the operator's age. A female amateur radio operator can be referred to as a YL, from the abbreviation used for "young lady", regardless of the operator's age.

XYL was once used by amateur radio operators to refer to an unlicensed woman, usually the wife of a male amateur radio operator; today, the term has come to mean any female spouse of an amateur radio operator, licensed or not. Although these codes are derived from English language abbreviations, their use is common among amateur radio operators worldwide. Incidentally, the most common language heard in the HF amateur bands (the bands below 30MHz that support worldwide communications) is English.

Age

In most countries there is no minimum age requirement to earn an amateur radio license and become an amateur radio operator. Although the number of amateur radio operators in many countries increases from year to year, the average age of amateur radio operators is quite high. In some countries, the average age is over 60 years old, with most amateur radio operators earning their license in their 40s or 50s.

Some national radio societies have responded to this by developing programs specifically to encourage youth participation in amateur radio, such as the American Radio Relay League's Amateur Radio Education and Technology Program. The World Wide Young Contesters organization promotes youth involvement, particularly amongst Europeans, in competitive radio contesting. A strong tie also exists between the amateur radio community and the Scouting movement to introduce radio technology to youth. WOSM's annual Jamboree On The Air is Scouting's largest activity, with a half million Scouts and Guides speaking with each other using amateur radio each October.

Citizens Band Radio

Citizens' band radio or CB is usually unlicensed broadcasting over frequencies set aside for that purpose. It is often used by truck drivers to communicate to one another.

Other Types of Radio Communication over Radiowaves

Radio communications have been and are used for all variety of data transmissions. The earliest radio application, Morse code, can still be heard today. Experiments in sending pictures and text date back to the early days of radio. A variety of clock signals are also broadcast. Another early use of radio was coded transmission of information by national governments in peace and war. During the Cold War the USSR and allied governments had national programs to block shortwave and other frequency transmissions by using jamming techniques. One signal known as Russian woodpecker suddenly appeared on July 4, 1976 and just as suddenly disappeared at the end of 1989, and is still something of a mystery. More and more radio frequencies are being used to send digital packets of information of varying degrees of complexity.

An early form of digital radio broadcasting was packet radio, which combines digital information with traditional radio broadcasting over the air. Digital radio broadcasting has emerged, first in Europe (the UK in 1995 and Germany in

1999), and later in the United States, France, the Netherlands, South Africa and many other countries worldwide. The most simple system is named DAB Digital Radio, for Digital Audio Broadcasting, and uses the public domain EUREKA 147 (Band III) system. DAB is used mainly in the UK and South Africa. Germany and Holland use the DAB and DAB+ systems, and France use the L-Band system of DAB Digital Radio.

In the United States digital radio isn't used in the same way as Europe and South Africa-instead the IBOC system is named HD Radio and owned by a consortium of private companies called biquity. An international non-profit consortium Digital Radio Mondiale (DRM), has introduced the public domain DRM system.

3

Television Journalism

History

In its early stages of development, television employed a combination of optical, mechanical and electronic technologies to capture, transmit and display a visual image. By the late 1920s, however, those employing only optical and electronic technologies were being explored.

All modern television systems rely on the latter, although the knowledge gained from the work on mechanical-dependent systems was crucial in the development of fully electronic television. The first time images were transmitted electrically were via early mechanical fax machines, including the pantelegraph, developed in the late 1800s.

The concept of electrically-powered transmission of television images in motion, was first sketched in 1878 as the telephonoscope, shortly after the invention of the telephone. At the time, it was imagined by early science fiction authors, that someday that light could be transmitted over wires, as sounds were. The idea of using scanning to transmit images was put to actual practical use in 1881 in the pantelegraph, through the use of a pendulum-based scanning mechanism.

From this period forward, scanning in one form or another, has been used in nearly every image transmission technology to date, including television. This is the concept of "rasterization", the process of converting a visual image into a stream of electrical pulses.

In 1884 Paul Gottlieb Nipkow, a 20-year old university student in Germany, patented the first electromechanical television system which employed a scanning disk, a spinning disk with a series of holes spiraling toward the centre, for rasterization. The holes were spaced at equal angular intervals such that in a single rotation the disk would allow light to pass through each hole and onto a light-sensitive selenium sensor which produced the electrical pulses. As an image was focused on the rotating disk, each hole captured a horizontal "slice" of the whole image, in a scanning fashion.

Nipkow's design would not be practical until advances in amplifier tube technology became available in 1907. Even then the device was only useful for transmitting still "halftone" images-represented by equally spaced dots of varying size-over telegraph or telephone lines. Later designs would use a rotating mirror-drum scanner to capture the image and a cathode ray tube (CRT) as a display device, but moving images were still not possible, due to the poor sensitivity of the selenium sensors.

Scottish inventor John Logie Baird demonstrated the transmission of moving silhouette images in London in 1925, and of moving, monochromatic images in 1926. Baird's scanning disk produced an image of 30 lines resolution, just enough to discern a human face, from a double spiral of lenses.. Remarkably, in 1927 Baird also invented the world's first video recording system, "Phonovision" — by modulating the output signal of his TV camera down to the audio range he was able to capture the signal on a 10-inch wax audio disc using conventional audio recording technology. A handful of Baird's 'Phonovision' recordings survive and these were finally decoded and rendered into viewable images in the 1990s using modern digital signal-processing technology.

In 1924 Hungarian engineer Kálmán Tihanyi invented a different image sensor technology: a metal plate with a mosaic of semiconductor elements in a vacuum tube. In 1926, Tihanyi patented his television system utilizing fully electronic scanning and display elements, and employing the principle of "charge storage" within the scanning (or "camera") tube.

By 1927, Russian inventor Léon Theremin developed a mirror drum-based television system which used interlacing to achieve an image resolution of 100 lines.

Also in 1927, Herbert E. Ives of Bell Labs transmitted moving images from a 50-aperture disk producing 16 frames per minute over a cable from Washington, DC to New York City, and via radio from Whippany, New Jersey. Ives used viewing screens as large as 24 by 30 inches (60 by 75 centimetres). His subjects included Secretary of Commerce Herbert Hoover.

In 1927, Philo Farnsworth made the world's first working television system with electronic scanning of both the pickup and display devices, which he first demonstrated to the press on 1 September 1928.

The first practical use of television was in Germany. Regular television broadcasts began in Germany in 1929 and in 1936 the Olympic Games in Berlin were broadcast to television stations in Berlin and Leipzig where the public could view the games live.

In 1936, Kálmán Tihanyi described the principle of plasma television, the first flat panel system.

Content

Programming

Getting TV programming shown to the public can happen in many different ways. After production the next step is to market and deliver the product to whatever markets are open to using it. This typically happens on two levels:

1. Original Run or First Run: a producer creates a program of one or multiple episodes and shows it on a station or network which has either paid for the production itself or to which a license has been granted by the producers to do the same.
2. Broadcast syndication: this is the terminology rather broadly used to describe secondary programming usages (beyond original run). It includes secondary runs in the

country of first issue, but also international usage which may or may not be managed by the originating producer. In many cases other companies, TV stations or individuals are engaged to do the syndication work, in other words to sell the product into the markets they are allowed to sell into by contract from the copyright holders, in most cases the producers.

First run programming is increasing on subscription services outside the U.S., but few domestically produced programs are syndicated on domestic free-to-air (FTA) elsewhere. This practice is increasing however, generally on digital-only FTA channels, or with subscriber-only first-run material appearing on FTA.

Unlike the U.S., repeat FTA screenings of a FTA network program almost only occur on that network. Also, affiliates rarely buy or produce non-network programming that is not centred around local events.

Funding

Around the globe, broadcast television is financed by either government, advertising, licensing (a form of tax), subscription or any combination of these. To protect revenues, subscription TV channels are usually encrypted to ensure that only subscription payers receive the decryption codes to see the signal. Non-encrypted channels are known as free to air or FTA.

Advertising

Television's broad reach makes it a powerful and attractive medium for advertisers. Many television networks and stations sell blocks of broadcast time to advertisers ("sponsors") in order to fund their programming.

United States

Since inception in the U.S. in 1940, TV commercials have become one of the most effective, persuasive, and popular method of selling products of many sorts, especially consumer goods. U.S. advertising rates are determined primarily by Nielsen Ratings. The time of the day and popularity of the channel determine how much a television commercial can cost. For example, the highly popular American Idol can cost approximately $750,000 for a thirty second block of commercial time; while the same amount of time for the World Cup and the Super Bowl can cost several million dollars.

In recent years, the paid program or infomercial has become common, usually in lengths of 30 minutes or one hour. Some drug companies and other businesses have even created "news" items for broadcast, known in the industry as video news releases, paying program directors to use them.

Some TV programs also weave advertisements into their shows, a practice begun in film and known as product placement. For example, a character could be drinking a certain kind of soda, going to a particular chain restaurant, or driving a certain make of car. (This is sometimes very subtle, where shows have vehicles provided by manufacturers for low cost, rather than wrangling them.) Sometimes a specific brand or trade mark, or music from a certain artist or group, is used. (This excludes guest appearances by artists, who perform on the show.)

United Kingdom

The TV regulator oversees TV advertising in the United Kingdom. Its restrictions have applied since the early days of commercially funded TV. Despite this, an early TV mogul, Lew Grade, likened the broadcasting licence as being a "licence to print money". Restrictions mean that the big three national commercial TV channels: ITV, Channel 4, and Five can show an average of only seven minutes of advertising per hour (eight minutes in the peak period). Other broadcasters must average no more than nine minutes (twelve in the peak). This means that many imported TV shows from the US have unnatural breaks where the UK company has edited out the breaks intended for US advertising. Advertisements must not be inserted in the course of certain specific proscribed types of programs which last less than half an hour in scheduled duration, this list includes any news or current affairs program, documentaries, and programs for children. Nor may advertisements be carried in a program designed and broadcast for reception in schools or in any religious service or other devotional program, or during a formal Royal ceremony or occasion. There also must be clear demarcations in time between the programs and the advertisements.

The BBC, being strictly non-commercial is not allowed to show advertisements on television in the UK, although it has many advertising-funded channels abroad. The majority of its budget comes from TV licencing and the sale of content to other broadcasters.

Republic of Ireland

The Broadcasting Commission of Ireland (BCI) (Irish: Coimisiún Craolacháin na hÉireann) oversees advertising on television and radio within the Republic of Ireland on both private and state owned broadcasters. Similar to other European countries, advertising is found on both private and state owned broadcasters. There are some restrictions based on advertising, especially in relation to the advertising of alcohol. Such advertisements are prohibited until after 7pm. Broadcasters in the Republic of Ireland adhere to broadcasting legislation implemented by the Broadcasting Commission of Ireland and the European Union. Sponsorship of current affairs programming is prohibited at all times.

As of October 1, 2009 the responsibilities held by the BCI are gradually being transferred to the Broadcasting Authority of Ireland.

Taxation or License

The BBC carries no advertising on its UK channels and is funded by an annual licence paid by all households owning a television. This licence fee is set by government, but the BBC is not answerable to or controlled by government and is therefore genuinely independent.

The two main BBC TV channels are watched by almost 90 percent of the population each week and overall have 27 per cent share of total viewing. This in spite of the fact that 85% of homes are multichannel, with 42% of these having access to 200 free to air channels via satellite and another 43% having access to 30 or more channels via Freeview. The licence that funds the seven advertising-free BBC TV channels currently costs £139.50 a year (about US$215) irrespective of the number of TV sets owned. When the same sporting event has been presented on both BBC and commercial channels, the BBC always attracts the lion's share of the audience, indicating viewers prefer to watch TV uninterrupted by advertising.

The Australian Broadcasting Corporation (ABC) carries no advertising (except for internal promotional material) as it is banned under the ABC Act 1983. The ABC receives its funding from the Australian Government every three years. In the 2008/09 Federal Budget the ABC received A$1.13 Billion. The funds assist in providing the ABC's Television, Radio, Online and International outputs. The ABC also receives funds from its many ABC Shops across Australia. However funded by the Australian Government the editorial independence of the ABC is ensured through law.

In France and the Republic of Ireland government-funded channels carry advertisements yet those who own television sets have to pay an annual tax ("la redevance audiovisuelle").

Subscription

Some TV channels are partly funded from subscriptions and therefore the signals are encrypted during broadcast to ensure that only paying subscribers have access to the decryption codes. Most subscription services are also funded by advertising.

Genres

Television genres include a broad range of programming types that entertain, inform, and educate viewers. The most expensive entertainment genres to produce are usually drama and dramatic miniseries. However, other genres, such as historical Western genres, may also have high production costs.

Popular entertainment genres include action-oriented shows such as police, crime, detective dramas, horror, or thriller shows. As well, there are also other variants of the drama genre, such as medical dramas and daytime soap operas. Science fiction shows can fall into either the drama or action category, depending on whether they emphasize philosophical questions or high adventure. Comedy is a popular genre which includes situation comedy (sitcom) and animated shows for the adult demographic such as Family Guy.

The least expensive forms of entertainment programming are game shows, talk shows, variety shows, and reality TV. Game shows show contestants answering questions and solving puzzles to win prizes. Talk shows feature interviews with film, television and music celebrities and public figures. Variety shows feature a range of musical performers and other entertainers such as comedians and magicians introduced by a host or Master of Ceremonies.

There is some crossover between some talk shows and variety shows, because leading talk shows often feature performances by bands, singers, comedians, and other performers in between the interview segments. Reality TV shows "regular" people (i.e., not actors) who are facing unusual challenges or experiences, ranging from arrest by police officers (COPS) to weight loss (The Biggest Loser). A variant version of reality shows depicts celebrities doing mundane activities such as going about their everyday life (Snoop Dogg's Father Hood) or doing manual labour.

Social Aspects

Television has played a pivotal role in the socialization of the 20th and 21st centuries. There are many aspects of television that can be addressed, including media violence research.

Environmental Aspects

With high lead content in CRTs, and the rapid diffusion of new, flat-panel display technologies, some of which (LCDs) use lamps containing mercury, there is growing concern about electronic waste from discarded televisions. Related occupational health concerns exist, as well, for disassemblers removing copper wiring and other materials from CRTs. Further environmental concerns related to television design and use relate to the devices' increasing electrical energy requirements.

Entertainment Industry

In 2001, film was accorded 'industry' status by the Indian Government this making it eligible for film financing from banks and financial institutions while the Industrial Development Bank of India (IDBI) set up the country's first film fund worth 100 crores. Cable television is the largest revenue earner with television broadcasting in second place and film third, followed closely by television production.

The future primary drivers for the entertainment industry will be growth in GDP, changes in demographic and the adoption of digital technology by the industry.

Negative Fallout: No excise duty on CD ROMs, but excise duty is levied on the audio CDs and video CDs although the manufacturing process, requirement of raw material and plant requirement for three types is the same. On top of it, a 4% excise duty as been imposed on MRP with regard to audiocassettes. No abatement has been offered with respect to this service tax on broadcast services.

In the entertainment segment, the films sector has been given the Industry status by the government. Estimates show that the entertainment industry is currently generating revenue of Rs. 100 billion and this will be able to increase by Rs. 315 billion by the year 2005. These measures include allowing listing to a company with 10% public ownership skin to the information technology industry. The FM radio broadcasting has been privatized. The current size of film segment, according to the latest estimate, is worth Rs. 22 billion. The average growth budget for the films has been increasing by 15% per annum.

Another high growth segment of the entertainment industry is the television broadcasting. The present size of this segment is estimated to be Rs. 35 billion.

The subscription revenues of the television channels are estimated to be around Rs. 25 billion currently. There are thirty five million households having access to about seventy channels the cable networks. The penetration of cable TV, particularly in the rural segment is expected to grow by 12% in the coming years.

The music industry is dominated by MC sales rather than CDs. The music industry in India is expected grow rate of 18-20% in the coming years.

TV And Film Production

Television viewing has now reached an all-time high in the United States. A 2009 report by the Nielsen Company says the average American television viewer is watching more than 151 hours of television per month— up from an average of 145 hours the previous year. Most U.S. homes receive about 120 channels.-*CNN*

Camerapersons, writers, directors, producers, and even on-camera talent find that having a solid understanding of the tools and techniques of the entire process makes a major difference in the success of productions— not to mention their careers. In television production, as in most of today's high-tech areas, knowledge is power.

A Bird's Eye View of the Production Process

Let's take a whirlwind tour of the production process. But unlike a whirlwind tour of Europe (if it's Tuesday, this must be Barcelona), we'll come back to these people and places later. For now, let's take a quick look at the production process from the standpoint of the key people. We'll start by thinking big — big productions, that is — because many of these things can be scaled down, combined, or eliminated in smaller productions.

Who Does What and Why

This list is long, but have you noticed the lengthy credit lists for major films and TV programs?

He or she comes up with the program concept, lays out the budget for the production, and makes the major decisions. This person is the team leader, the one who works with the writers, hires the director, decides on the key talent, and guides the general direction of the production.

In smaller productions, the producer may also take charge of the more mundane activities. And in small productions, the director may handle the producer's responsibilities. In this case, the combined job title becomes (want to guess?), producer-director.

Some productions may also have an associate producer who sets up schedules for the talent and crew and who generally assists the producer.

On a major production, one of the producer's first jobs is to hire a writer to write the script (the document that tells everyone what to do and say). The script is like a written plan or blueprint for the production.

The producer will next consider the key talent for the production. In general, the talent includes actors, reporters, hosts, guests, and off-camera narrators — anyone whose voice is heard or who appears on camera.

Sometimes talent is broken down into three sub-categories: actors (who portray other people in dramatic productions), performers (who appear on camera in nondramatic roles), and announcers (who generally don't appear on camera).

The director is in charge of working out *preproduction* (before the production) details, coordinating the activities of the production staff and on-camera talent, working out camera and talent positions on the set, selecting the camera shots during production, and supervising *postproduction* (after production) work.

In other words, once the producer sets things in motion, the director is in charge of taking the script from the beginning to the very end of the production process.

Assisting a director in the control room is typically a technical director who operates the video switcher. (A rather elaborate version is shown on the right.) The technical director, or TD, is also responsible for coordinating the technical aspects of the production.

One or more production assistants (PAs) may be hired to help the producer and director. Among other things, PAs keep notes on ongoing production needs and changes. The lighting director (LD) designs the lighting plan, arranges for the lighting equipment, and sets up and checks the lighting.

As we'll see, lighting is a key element in the overall look of a production.

Some productions have a set designer who, along with the producer and director, designs the set and supervises its construction, painting, and installation.

The makeup person, with the help of cosmetics, hair spray, etc., sees that the talent look their best — or their worst, if that's what the script calls for.

Makeup is just one of the areas where a link will take you to advanced information. (We'll discuss the meaning of the coloured squares below).

It should be emphasized that specific responsibilities of production personnel will vary widely, depending on the production facility. In Europe, and in particular at the BBC (British Broadcasting System) in London, these distinctions are made.

Let's resume our list of the important people involved in TV production.

Major dramatic productions have a wardrobe person who sees that the actors have clothes appropriate to the story and script.

The audio director or audio technician arranges for the audio recording equipment, sets up and checks mics (microphones), monitors audio quality during the production, and then strikes (another production term meaning disassembles and, if necessary, removes) the audio recording equipment and accessories after the production is over.

The microphone boom/grip operator watches rehearsals and decides on the proper mics and their placement for each scene. During an on-location (out-of-the-studio) shoot, this person may need strong arms to hold the mic boom over the talent for long periods of time.

The video recorder operator arranges video recording equipment and accessories, sets up video recordings, performs recording checks, and monitors video quality.

In dramatic productions, the continuity secretary (CS) carefully makes notes on scene and continuity details as each scene is shot to ensure that these details remain consistent among takes and scenes.

As we will see, this is a much more important job than you might think, especially in single-camera, on-location production. Once production concerns are taken care of, the continuity secretary is responsible for releasing the actors after each scene or segment is shot.

We're almost done with our list. Are you still with us? The CG Operator, (electronic character generator operator) programs (designs/types in) opening titles, subtitles, and closing credits into a computer-based device that inserts the text over the video.

Camera operators do more than just operate cameras. They typically help set up the cameras and ensure their technical quality, and they work with the director, lighting director, and audio technician in blocking (setting up) and shooting each shot.

On a field (out-of-the-studio, or on-location) production, they may also coordinate camera equipment pickup and delivery.

Depending on the production, there may be a floor manager or stage manager who's responsible for coordinating activities on the set. One or more floor persons, or stagehands, may assist him or her.

After shooting is completed, the editors use the video and audio recordings to blend the segments together. Technicians add music and audio effects to create the final product.

The importance of editing to the success of a production is far greater than most people realize. As we will see, an editor can make or break a production. This finishes the list of people and what they do. We'll revisit these as we go along, so don't worry if you don't remember them all at this point.

The Three Production Phases

The production process is commonly broken down into preproduction, production, and postproduction, which some people roughly characterize as "before, during, and after."

The Preproduction Phase

The importance of this is often more fully appreciated after things get pretty well messed up during a production and the production people look back and wish they had adhered to this axiom from the start.

In preproduction the basic ideas and approaches of the production are developed and set in motion. It is in this phase that the production can be set on a proper course or misdirected (messed up) to such an extent that no amount of time, talent, or editing expertise can save it.

Hit the Target Audience

In order for the program to be successful, you must keep in mind throughout each production phase the needs, interests, and general background of the target audience (the audience your production is designed to reach).

In order for your program to have value and a lasting effect, it must in some way affect the audience emotionally.

This assumes both knowledge of the prime directive and the target audience, and it ends up being a key to your personal success.

During preproduction, not only are key talent and production members selected, but all the major elements are planned. Since things such as scenic design, lighting, and audio are interrelated, they must be carefully coordinated in a series of production meetings.

A simple on-location segment may involve only a quick check of talent positions so that camera moves, audio, and lighting can be checked.

A complex dramatic production may require many days of rehearsals. These generally start with a table reading or dry rehearsal where the talent along with key production personnel sit around a table and read through the script. Often, script changes take place at this point.

Finally, there's a dress rehearsal. Here, the talent dresses in the appropriate wardrobe, and all production elements are in place. This is the final opportunity for production personnel to solve whatever production problems remain.

The Production Phase

The production phase is where everything comes together (we can hope) in a kind of final performance.

Productions can be broadcast either *live* or *recorded.* With the exception of news shows, sports remotes, and some special-event broadcasts, productions are typically recorded for later broadcast or distribution.

Recording the show or program segment provides an opportunity to fix problems by either making changes during the editing phase or stopping the recording and redoing a segment.

And, Finally, the Postproduction Phase

Tasks, such as striking (taking down) sets, dismantling and packing equipment, handling final financial obligations, and evaluating the effect of the program, are part of the postproduction phase.

Even though postproduction includes all of these after-the-production jobs, most people associate postproduction with editing.

As computer-controlled editing techniques and postproduction special effects have become more sophisticated, editing has gone far beyond the original concept of simply joining segments in a desired order. Editing is now a major focus of production creativity.

Armed with the latest digital effects, the editing phase can add much in the way of razzmatazz to a production. In fact, it's pretty easy to become enthralled with the special effect capabilities of your equipment.

Confusing the Medium with the Message

As fun as all the razzmatazz effects might be to play with, you should consider all this high-tech stuff merely a tool for a greater purpose: the effective communication of ideas and information.

If that sounds a bit academic and stuffy, you might want to look at things from a broader timeline. If you think about it, today's latest high-tech effects will look pretty lame a few years from now.

It's only the ideas and feelings that have a chance of enduring.

How many times have you seen a movie and forgotten about it almost as soon as you left the theatre? In contrast, some movies seem to "stick with you," and you may think about them for days or even weeks.

In 2005, the average American spent about 1,700 hours watching television, the equivalent of 70 full days. The average U.S. home has more TV sets than people.

The medium you are learning to control can be used either to provide audiences with time-wasting, mindless, drivel......or with ideas that can make a positive difference in the overall scheme of things. (And, as you may have noticed, there is a definite need in the world for people who can make a positive difference.)

How would you rather have your work and life remembered?

Program Proposals and Treatments

Now that you know who does what and you have an overview of the basic production process, let's move on to the actual process of doing a TV production.

Even though you may have a clear idea in your head of what you want to get across in a production, unless you can clearly communicate that idea to the people who can help you launch your production, that's just where your idea will stay—in your head.

These people include the producer, director, production crew, sponsor, and, most importantly, your audience.

So where do you start?

Writing the Program Proposal or Treatment

The first step in a complex production is to write a clear and succinct summary of your ideas.

We refer to this summary as a treatment in dramatic productions and a program proposal in nondramatic productions.

A Sample Program Proposal for a Local TV Station

Sample Program Proposal

"Underwater Explorations" will be a weekly, 30-minute studio production featuring guests supplying their own video or film footage of their underwater exploits around the world.

The proposed host for the show is Dr. Steve Adams, who has an established track record with us and WCFX-TV for doing marine specials. Each week he will have a new guest with new experiences.

Given the numerous people within our seacoast broadcast area who regularly document their diving expeditions, we will have no trouble finding guests with exciting footage and stories to tell. In particular we want to feature in-studio close-ups of artifacts that have been salvaged during underwater expeditions.

Two guests who have documented the discovery of sunken ships are interested in appearing. In addition, we want to feature experts in marine life from the local university who have dramatic and colorful digital footage of a wide variety of underwater life forms.

Dave's Dive Shop and Marty's Marine Supply have tentatively committed as sponsors. Numerous other potential sponsors also exist within our broadcast area.

Production costs would be minimal. The production could be done "live-on-tape" on Wednesday evenings in Studio B with three cameras — one typically reserved for tabletop close-ups of exhibits. Dr. Adams indicates he would be willing to host/produce the show for $950 per program. Our initial contract with Dr. Adams would be for 13 shows.

Although the guests would appear without compensation, the potential sponsors have indicated that they would give the guests gifts in exchange for on-air acknowledgments.

The Sunday afternoon broadcast time slot now occupied by What In the World, (which concludes April 2nd,) seems most appropriate, although the final decision on this would be up to Programming.

Get Agreement on Your Proposal

Getting the go-ahead on a proposal affords everyone a bit of insurance. Once everyone agrees on the treatment or program proposal, it's difficult for someone to say later, "This isn't what we agreed on."

This is especially important in large production facilities and television networks, where a variety of people will be involved in program development.

A simple program proposal may be just a couple of pages or, in the case of a feature-length dramatic production, a treatment can run 60 pages or more.

This is as good a place as any to mention the importance of *writing*.

Yes, I know, you've heard that since you were in fourth grade.

There may even be some people out there who decided to go into TV (rather than print journalism, for example) because they thought they might be able to escape having to learn how to write.

Sorry.

Although it's a visual medium, TV is still based on the written word. When you get down to it, your ability to write and effectively communicate your ideas ends up being the most important criterion for success. Unless you want to stick with the very basic jobs in TV, you have to face this reality — and the sooner the better.

Interestingly, most producers (the people in charge, remember?) arrived at their jobs by first being writers.

Wouldn't you rather end up being someone who makes the major decisions (and is paid accordingly)?

Okay, back to treatments and program proposals.

Although we write them as an aid in presenting and getting agreement on the focus and direction of the production, they are also used to interest key people in supporting the production— especially financial backers.

See that Your Proposal Engages the Audience's Interest and Imagination

A program proposal or treatment should cover the essence of the production; or, in the case of a dramatic production, the basic story line.

Dramatic treatments also include the locations and talent required, as well as the key scenes.

In nondramatic program proposals the basic production needs and approximate times of the segments are included.

Anyone reading a program proposal or treatment should be able to get a clear idea of the entire production.

If disagreement exists on the program concept, it's much easier to change things at this stage than after the complete script is written.

Writing A Treatment

A treatment consists of a written condensation of a proposed film or TV dramatic production. It covers the basic ideas and issues of the production as well as the main characters, locations, and story angles.

In part, its purpose is to sell the proposal to financial backers and major stars. Treatments should be attention-getting and interesting to read. They are written in the present tense, and often read like a short story. Treatments cover the full story sequence. They typically contain some key scenes (script dialogue that is, or will be, in the script).

There is typically one treatment page for every two script pages. Using this rule a treatment for a feature-length dramatic production would run about 60 pages. Even so, many treatments are much shorter than this.

Capturing and Holding Viewer Attention

It would be difficult to think of any business that's more competitive than TV broadcasting. The average viewer in the United States has dozens of TV channels from which to choose.

Each year, the TV industry spends millions of dollars trying to make successful new TV shows. And each year most of these attempts don't even make it to air (broadcast).

First, get their Attention!

The success of a TV show (and, therefore, your own professional success) will depend in large measure on your ability to effectively capture and hold an audience.

And, once you do, you'd better have something interesting to communicate or they'll quickly go elsewhere — either tuning to another channel or just mentally tuning you out.

"But," you say, "I don't want to worry about all that; I just want to make TV shows that interest me."

That's great, but who's going to pay for them?

Reality 101

TV productions cost a lot of money, especially today. To cite just one example, in 1966 the budget for each full episode of Star Trek was $100,000. In 2003, each episode of Enterprise, which is similar in form, cost about $100,000 per minute to produce. Today, the cost would be even higher.

Before people put up that kind of money, they have to believe there will be some kind of return on their investment.

Depending on the type of production, that return may be to communicate a corporate message effectively, to get viewers to understand a series of concepts or, in the case of commercial television, to generate profits by selling products.

Hit the Target (Audience)

As we've noted, we use the term target audience to indicate the specific segment of a potential audience we're "aiming at."

Regardless of the type of production, you must start with a clear understanding of the needs and interests of your specific target audience.

Advertisers spend millions of dollars determining these things.

Depending on the products they want to sell, advertisers will have certain demographic preferences.

For designer jeans, for example, the target audience would be fairly affluent teenagers. The same advertisers wouldn't be interested in sponsoring reruns of Murder, She Wrote, which appeals primarily to an older audience.

By the way, the principles of determining the needs and interests of your target audience also apply to something as simple as producing a video for your class. If only an instructor will be evaluating your video, you'll probably take a different approach than if it's intended for a graduation party. In either case, meeting the needs of your target audience is the key to success.

Let's look at just a few of the issues involved.

Using Audience-Engaging Techniques

Although people may want to believe they're being completely logical in evaluating a program, their underlying emotional reaction most influences their evaluation. Even a logical, educational presentation evokes — for better or worse— an emotional response.

This is a key concept, which Benjamin Franklin (a noted persuader) put this way:

If you would persuade, you must appeal to interest rather than intellect.

Benjamin Franklin

What types of production content are most apt to engage our interest and affect us emotionally?

First, we have an interest in other people, especially in "experiencing the experiences" of other people.

We're interested in people who lead interesting (romantic, dangerous, wretched, or engrossingly spiritual) lives.

Part of this involves gaining new insights and being exposed to new points of view. This includes learning new things.

Here's something else to keep in mind.

Viewers like content that reinforces their existing attitudes and, right or wrong, they tend to react against ideas that run contrary to their beliefs.

Production people, therefore, must be careful in presenting ideas that blatantly challenge widely held beliefs.

The trick is to know how far you can go without alienating an audience.

To cite a rather extreme example, a number of years ago an East Coast TV station did an exposé on a local police chief. An undercover reporter (one of my former students, in fact) put a camera in a lunch box and filmed the police chief clearly taking a bribe.

When the segment was broadcast, there was negative reaction — against the TV station.

It seems the police chief was popular with many influential people in the community and having the truth presented in this way challenged their commitment to this individual. This reaction on the part of many viewers was justified by cries of entrapment, a liberal media bias against a law-and-order official, etc.

The same negative anti-media reaction took place when former U.S. President Richard Nixon was forced to resign from office for engaging in illegal activities while in the White House. To see how this came about, rent the Academy Award winning feature-length film, All the President's Men. The film represents an important piece of U.S. history presented in a dramatic and even exciting way. It also illustrates how two tenacious reporters faced down major high-level opposition to expose wrongdoing.

Eventually, this U.S. president had to resign. The reporters involved kept the identity of "Deep Throat," the inside informer involved, secret for several decades.

If a democracy is to be successful, the news media have a *social responsibility* to ring ruth to light — even though that truth may be unpopular.

Audiences also like to hear about things that are new and that generate excitement. This is why mystery, sex, fear, violence, and horror do so well at the box office.

It also explains why we see so many car chases, explosions, and general instances of mayhem in our films and TV programs.

Such things stir our adrenaline and involve us emotionally. In short, they hold our attention.

This, of course, brings up the possibility of exploitation, presenting things that appeal to elements of human nature that — how shall we say this — aren't the most positive.

Sometimes a rather blurry line exists between honestly presenting ideas and stories, and unduly emphasizing elements such as sex and violence just for the sake of grabbing and holding an audience.

Beyond a certain point, audiences will sense they're being exploited and manipulated, and resent it.

And, keep in mind, the content of a production, good or bad, tends to rub off on the reputations of those who produce it — and even on the sponsors who support it.

With this general background on programming elements that appeal to audiences, we'll next turn to the production sequence. Some people say that the media and the arts have too much freedom and that the range of ideas presented by the media — which primarily means broadcast television — should be more tightly controlled.

Given the present climate we need to remind ourselves that the success of a democratic society is based on an informed electorate; and the only way to have an informed electorate is to allow a free flow of information.

A nation that is afraid to let its people judge the truth and falsehood of ideas in an open market is a nation that is afraid of its people. John F. Kennedy, former U.S. President (D)

Although we all learned about such things in our civics classes, today these values are easy to forget—especially when the free flow of information contains ideas that go against our basic beliefs.

Some cases in point: the patently absurd headlines and stories regularly appearing in tabloids ("Two-Headed Woman Marries Two Men!"); some of the U.S. TV programs that have pushed tabloid journalism to new heights; and, of course, the photos, films, videotapes, and art work that have been branded by some as "pornographic."

Censorship for the Sake of Our Values

These and other seeming abuses of free speech have been enough to make many people cry for some type of control of the media—some type of censorship.

And that's exactly what's been happening.

According to USA Today, overt moves to censor books take place in about 20 percent of U.S. schools each year, with unreported efforts far exceeding this percent.

Things that have been censored in the United States include Shakespeare's plays, and such classic books as: The Red Badge of Courage, Mr. Roberts, Catcher in the Rye, the Great Gatsby, The Adventures of Huckleberry Finn, To Kill a Mockingbird, Lord of the Flies, 1984, Go Ask Alice, Of Mice and Men, the Tarzan books, and the Harry Potter books.

The Harry Potter books (responsible for turning on thousands of young people to reading) have been banned by some conservative religious groups that feel that they are associated with witchcraft. In fact, the Potter books were the most censored books in 2002.

Even Webster's New World Dictionary has been banned in some schools because it contains "objectionable words."

Interestingly, one of the most disdained fascists in history, Adolf Hitler, won popular approval by promising to clean up "moral corruption" in the media of his time.

Once he gained control of Germany, he was directly or indirectly responsible for the death of:

- 6 million Jews
- 9 million East Europeans
- 20 million Soviet citizens
- 4 million German soldiers (2 million in the course of his "ethnic cleansing")
- 1 million Western Allied soldiers.

Then, as now, the idea of "cleaning up the media" can have great popular appeal.

Censorship has not only been taking place in our schools. During the last decade or so, attempts to keep certain governmental activities from the public have reached new heights.

The percentage of government documents marked "classified" has dramatically increased. Many classified documents have nothing to do with national security — they include toxic-waste studies and significant findings on occupational hazards.

More recently, of course, the Internet has become a focus for censorship. In the old days when a messenger gave a king bad news, the king would sometimes become so upset he would kill the messenger. Today, we often see anger directed against today's messengers, the news media.

Although the news media is justifiably blamed for many excesses, those of us who have worked in news know how readily corruption can thrive when it can be hidden from public disclosure. But thanks to communication technology, it's not nearly as easy to hide things today.

To cite just one example, using today's high-quality camcorders, concerned citizens have documented a wide range of abuses of the public trust. We've seen some of the results on network news and public affairs programming.

Even cell phone camera videos often end up on sites such as YouTube and occasionally even end up on network and cable news programs.

Despots who fear losing their position of authority are generally quick to initiate censorship.

The more insecure their status the more desperate their efforts.

Throughout history totalitarian regimes and censorship have gone hand in hand.

From a psychological perspective there is a demonstrable relationship between psychological security and tolerance.

Put another away, personal insecurities are often related to an inability to tolerate new ideas or ideas that run contrary to our own.

Insecurity and the inability to confront new ideas are related to the mobilization of four mental mechanisms.

Personal Defense Mechanisms

First is selective exposure, where individuals try to minimize exposure to ideas that run contrary to their own beliefs. In this way their views have little chance of being challenged or changed— even though important new facts may emerge.

Those who try to limit their own exposure (or other people's exposure) to new ideas may be creating a situation that actually works against them in the long run.

Studies — especially those associated with brainwashing— indicate that people who do not have a chance to compare and defend their ideas are most apt to abandon them when they are confronted with an opposing view — even though that opposing view is unsound.

However, those who have had ample opportunity to test and defend their views are most likely to hold on to them when they are challenged.

Interestingly, some radio talk show hosts screen their guests so that no one who holds a view contrary to their own will be featured on the show.

Rather than welcome the chance to confront what they think is an inferior idea and stimulate thinking, they seem to fear such ideas. Thus, you can often tell how a secure a person is in their personal beliefs by how well they tolerate opposing beliefs.

The Incestuous Amplification Effect discusses an important aspect of this.

The second defense mechanism is selective perception. In this case when individuals are presented with ideas or data that contradict their beliefs, they refuse to "see" or recognize the information.

If, despite their efforts, they have to confront these ideas, the individuals may try to discredit the source, or attribute the ideas to an incompetent, corrupt, biased, or evil source.

In a Stanford study, 48 students, half of whom said they favored capital punishment and half of whom said they opposed it, were presented with two pieces of evidence, one supporting and one contradicting the claim that capital punishment deters crime. In a follow-up check of attitudes both groups were convinced that all of the evidence presented supported their initial position.

Finally, there is source amnesia. For this we need to consider how memory works.

A fact is first stored in the hippocampus of the brain, but each time we recall it, our brain "writes it down again." During this "rewriting," the central fact is gradually transferred to the cerebral cortex and is frequently separated from the original context or source. We know we "heard it," but we don't recall if it was a rumour circulated on the Internet or from a talk radio caller, or it was from a respected source, such as a medical journal. As the source is forgotten, what was at first may have been recognized as rumour or fiction, takes on credibility.

Adding to source amnesia is the previously discussed *selective recall* where our memory holds onto to ideas that support or beliefs and forgets crucial facts that don't.

How does this relate to the production of news and documentary productions?

First, documentary and news writers may assume that they can use experts to attack information that is not true. However, by repeating the false information, they may inadvertently reinforce the false concept.

Many celebrities do not sue tabloids when they print blatantly false information because the act will bring the false information — especially if it's scandalous information — to the attention of people, who, thereafter will forget that it was proven false.

If you wanted to dispel the idea that the sun does not revolve around the earth, for example, which 18 percent of people believe, you would not just say, "the sun does not revolve around the sun" and bring up the image of the sun revolving around the earth in people's minds. With time, some listeners would only remember "sun revolves around the earth." Truth would be better served by saying *and illustrating* how, "the earth revolves around the sun."

Limited Ability to Make Essential Adjustments

Although these defense mechanisms tend to protect our belief systems, they also limit our growth and personal opportunities.

Possibly more importantly, they limit our ability to adjust to changing needs by being able to consider new solutions to problems.

Throughout history we've seen what happens to species and societies that were not capable of adequately adapting to change. Today, change is assuming an ever-accelerating pace.

Part of this change involves the emergence of ideas that are new—even ideas that threaten cherished beliefs.

At one time it was heresy to suggest that the world was not flat or not at the centre of the universe. Those who were bold enough to openly advocate another view were censored or even tortured until they "repented." And if that didn't work, they were simply killed, "for the good of society and their souls."

The Price of Freedom

Sometimes we must defend the rights of those we disagree with in order to insure that we, ourselves, will retain the freedom to share ideas that we consider better and more worthy.

No, freedom and values are not in conflict as long as we are personally strong enough to consider alternative views and make informed choices based on the knowledge that this freedom makes possible.

In Germany they came first for the Communists, and I didn't speak up, because I was not a Communist.

The Production Sequence

Let's think big — as in a big production: Following are 15 basic steps required for an elaborate television production. Once you get a feel for the entire process, you can scale things down for any sized production.

Identify the Purpose of the Production

This is the most important step: Clearly identify the production's goals and purposes. If there is no clear agreement on the goals and purposes of a production, it will be impossible to evaluate its success. (How will you know if you've arrived at your destination, if you didn't know where you were going in the first place?) Is the purpose to instruct, inform, or entertain— or maybe to generate feelings of pride or express a social, religious, or political need? Is the real purpose to create a desire in the audience to take some action?

Let's be honest. The primary goal of most broadcasting is simply to hold the interest of an audience through the intervening commercials.

Most productions have more than one goal and we'll elaborate on some of these later.

Analyze Your Target Audience

Next, identify and analyze your target audience. Based on such things as age, sex, socioeconomic status, and educational level, program content preferences will differ.

These preferences are also different in various regions of the United States (e.g., North, South, urban, rural). As we've noted, we refer to audience characteristics as demographics.

We can see regional demographic variations, in part, by differences in local programming in various areas of the country — and sometimes by the films and network programming that local stations decide not to air. Sex and violence are chief among these content issues — and both show a positive relationship to ratings.

Identify Demographics to Determine the Acceptability of Content

Knowing your audience, of course, is crucial to success — and not understanding it is at the base of many failures. Let's look at some examples.

Generally speaking — and, of course, there are many exceptions — when it comes to sexual themes, people living in Northern urban areas of the United States tend to be more tolerant than people who have a rural background and live in the South. Education is also related. Research shows that, generally, the more educated the audience, the less they object to sexual themes.

Interestingly, it appears that this relationship seems to be the reverse when it comes to violence: More educated audiences are less tolerant of violence in the media.

Knowing that more than 41,000 women are diagnosed with breast cancer in the United States each year, a female program manager of a TV station in the South decided to run a PSA (public service announcement) on the importance of doing breast self-examinations.

Even though the PSA ran late at night and may have seemed rather bland in its approach, there was immediate negative reaction on the part of some members of the audience who thought the subject matter was too personal to be broadcast. Because of viewer complaints, the station canceled the PSA, depriving the public of valuable cancer prevention information.

In 2006, a similar controversy broke out over a vaccination that can prevent cervical cancer, which kills more than 3,500 women in the United States each year. Some social conservatives both oppose its use and the dissemination of pro-vaccination information. Although the vaccine would save thousands of lives, cervical cancer is associated with sexual activity and these people feel the vaccination could encourage premarital sex.

With strong pressures on each side of controversial issues, broadcasters have to try to sort out fact from fiction and try to follow their legal mandate of 'operating in the public's interest, convenience and necessity.'

At the same time, what is and is not broadcast is largely determined by audience feedback and this can varies greatly with demographics. For example, in contrast to the relatively innocuous PSA on breast cancer we mentioned, some PBS stations have run programming with brief full frontal nudity late at night without appreciable reaction.

The difference? Demographics. The people most apt to complain weren't watching, and the people watching were least apt to complain.

You may have a compulsion to "just tell it like it is" and not be concerned about alienating your audience.

Time to review those Reality 101 notes. If you consistently disregard audience preferences and predispositions, you'll limit your future in TV production. But what if you're not producing programming for broadcast or general distribution? Compared to standard broadcast television, institutional television, which includes corporate and educational video, has different needs and expectations. But here too, predominating demographic characteristics, such as age, sex, and education, influence a production's form and content.

For example, to underestimate education or experience and inadvertently "talk down to" an audience insults them. To overestimate education or experience and talk over people's heads is just as bad. Either way, you lose.

Check out Similar Productions

Check out similar productions from the past. If you're going to make mistakes, at least make new ones. Ask yourself some questions: How will your proposed production differ from previous successful and unsuccessful efforts by others? Why did they work; or, maybe more importantly, why didn't they? Of course, since production styles change rapidly, you need to take into consideration differences in time, locations, and audiences.

Determine the Basic Value of Your Production

Next, determine the overall value of the production to a sponsor or underwriter. Obviously, underwriters and advertisers want some sort of return on their investment. (Reality 101 rears its head again!)

Although we'll cover costing out a production later, here we want to make certain we can justify production expenses in terms of a gain or *return on the investment* (*ROI*).

For this, you'll need to ask yourself some questions. First, what is the probable size of the audience? In determining this, you must know if your show will be a one-shot presentation or if you can recoup production expenses over time by presenting the show to other audiences.

Generally, the larger the audience the more marketable a production will be to an underwriter or advertiser. At the same time, simple numbers don't tell the full story. Let's say an advertiser has a product designed for young people — athletic shoes or designer jeans. In this case, a production that draws a large percentage of this age group will be more valuable than a production that has a larger overall audience, but a lower percentage of young people.

Broadcasters have canceled many TV series, *not* because they had a small audience, but because they had the *wrong kind* of audience (the wrong demographics).

Consider Return on Investment

You'll always want to balance the potential value of a production to an advertiser or underwriter with the projected cost of producing and presenting the production.

If the costs exceed the benefits, you have a problems!

In commercial television, the ROI is generally in the form of increased sales and profits. But it may take other forms, such as the expected moral, political, spiritual, or public relations benefit derived from the program.

Develop a Treatment or Production Proposal

Next, put it down on paper. The steps involved span the interval from the initial proposal to the final shooting script. You'll recall that earlier we talked about treatments and program proposals (written summaries of what you propose to do). After the program proposal or treatment is approved, you'll submit— on request — a full script. (Remember, we're talking about a major production.)

It will be at this point that any remaining research on the content will be commissioned.

During these sessions, you and others will thrash out such things as audience appeal, pace, and problems with special interest groups, and you'll consider alternative ideas.

If it's an institutional production, you'll review the production's goals and pose questions about the most effective ways to present ideas. If the director is on board at this time, he or she should be part of these conferences. Finally, a script version emerges that is (we can hope) more or less acceptable to everyone. Even this version, however, will probably not be final. In many instances, scene revisions continue right up to the time the scenes are shot.

Typically, in a dramatic film production, each new script version is issued on a different colour paper so that the cast and crew won't confuse them with earlier versions. ("Margaret, wake up; you're still going by the pink pages, and we're on yellow!")

Depending on the production, you may want to develop a storyboard.

A storyboard consists of drawings of key scenes with corresponding notes on elements such as dialogue, sound effects, and music.

Develop a Production Schedule

Next, draw up a tentative schedule. Generally, broadcast or distribution deadlines will dictate the production schedule (the written timetable listing the time allotted for each production step). Not planning things out carefully might cause you to miss a critical deadline, rendering the production useless.

Select Key Production Personnel

Bring on board the remaining above-the-line production personnel. In addition to the producer and writer, above-the-line personnel include the production manager, director and, in general, key creative team members. Below-the-line personnel, generally assigned later, include the technical staff.

Decide on Locations

If you're not shooting in the studio, decide on key locations. In a major production you will hire a location scout or location manager to find and coordinate the use of the locations suggested by the script.

Although it might be easier to shoot in a TV studio, it's been shown that audiences like the authenticity of "real" locations, especially in dramatic productions. Most major cities encourage TV and film production and maintain film commissions that supply photos and videotapes of interesting shooting locations in their area. They'll also provide information on usage fees and the names of people to contact.

It's often necessary to make changes in the on-location settings. For instance, rooms may have to be repainted or redecorated and visible signs changed.

Decide on Talent, Wardrobe and Sets

Next, you'll want to make some decisions on talent, wardrobe (costuming) and sets.

Depending on the type of production, auditions may take place at this point as part of the casting process (selecting people for the various roles).

If you're lucky enough to afford well-known actors, you'll probably have decided on them early in the preproduction process.

Once you decide on the talent, you can begin wardrobe selection. These are suggested by the script, coordinated with the look of the sets and locations, and ultimately approved by the director.

After a set designer is hired, he or she will review the script, possibly do research, and then discuss initial ideas with the director.

Once there's agreement, sketches of the sets can be made for final approval before actual set construction starts — if there is any construction. Today, many sets exist only in computers and the actors are electronically inserted into them. If this is the case, the set sketches will be given to a computer artist.

You can then schedule rehearsals, from initial table readings to the final dress rehearsal.

Even though personnel may not have finished the sets at this point, the actors can start reading through the script with the director to establish pace, emphasis, and basic blocking (the positioning of sets, furniture, cameras, and actors). Once the sets are finished, the final blocking and dress rehearsals can get underway.

Decide on the Remaining Production Personnel

Make decisions on the remaining staff and production needs. At this point you can arrange for key technical personnel, equipment, and facilities. This includes the rental of both equipment and production facilities.

Next, arrange transportation, catering (food and refreshment trucks) and on-location accommodations.

Unions, which may or may not be involved, often set minimum standards for transportation, as well as the quality of meals and accommodations. Union contracts also cover job descriptions, specific crew responsibilities and working hours, including graduated pay increases for overtime hours.

Obtain Permits, Insurance, and Clearances

In major cities and in many foreign countries it's not possible just to go to the location of your choice, set up your tripod, and start filming. Except for spot news and short documentary segments, you must arrange access permits, licenses, security bonds, and insurance policies.

Many semipublic interior locations, such as shopping malls, require filming permits. (Yes, these things do get complicated!)

Depending on the nature of the production, *liability insurance* and *security bonds* may be necessary because accidents can happen that can be directly or indirectly attributed to the production. In some locations, the controlling agency will limit exterior production to certain areas and specific hours. In a street scene where traffic will be affected you'll need to arrange for special police.

We also include in this category a wide variety of clearances, ranging from permission to using prerecorded music to reserving satellite time to transmit the production back to a studio. If you can't obtain clearance, you need time to explore alternatives.

Are you beginning to see why list of credits in films and TV programs is so long?

Select Video Inserts, Still Photos, and Graphics

Arrange to shoot or acquire videotape and film inserts, still photos, and graphics.

To reduce production costs, check out existing stock footage in film and tape libraries around the country. This is generally background footage, such as general exterior scenes of an area that will be edited into the production.

Second unit work is production done away from the main location by a separate production crew and generally does not involve the principal, on-camera talent.

If part of a dramatic production calls for shots of a specific building in Cleveland, for example, a second unit can shoot the necessary exteriors in Cleveland while the primary unit works on interior shots (which are supposedly taking place inside the building) in Southern California where the actors live.

You will want to begin to make decisions on music at this point, including working out copyright clearances and royalties for music and visual inserts. We'll discuss these in more detail later.

Begin Rehearsals and Shooting

Start rehearsing and shooting. Depending on the type of production, rehearsals may take place either minutes or days before the actual shooting.

Begin Editing Phase

After shooting is completed, the producer, director, and video recording editor review the footage and start to make editing decisions. This has typically been done in two phases: on-line and off-line.

Briefly, in off-line editing copies of the original taped footage that contains time-code number references are used to develop a kind of blueprint for final editing. In on-line editing the original footage is used in editing. During the final editing phase, sound sweetening (enhancing), colour balancing, and special effects are added.

Because editing is so important to the creative process, we're going to devote several chapters to the subject.

If all these terms and procedures sound a bit intimidating right now, don't worry; we'll explain them in more detail later.

Do Postproduction Follow-up

Although most of the production crew will conclude their work by the time production wraps (finishes), some follow-up work generally needs to be completed.

Included is totaling up financial statements, paying the final bills, and determining the production's success (or failure). Ratings indicate success levels in broadcast television. In institutional television success may be determined by testing, program evaluations, and viewer feedback.

Ratings, Shares, HUTS, and CPM

Each of the above factors is important in determining the success of a program or commercial.

Rating-A rating is the percentage of households tuned to a particular program from the total available TV households in a designated area.

In this example there are 500 households tuned to program "A" out of a possible 2,800 (all of the TV households represented in the pie).

By dividing the larger number (2,800) into the smaller (500) we get a percent; in this case 17.86. So the rating of program "A" is 18. (Since ratings are in terms of percentages, you don't need to say "percent," just 18.) Using the same procedure you can see that the rating for program "B" would be 11.

Share-A share is the percentage of TV households with sets turned on that are watching your program. In the case of program "A" you divide 1,600 into 500 and get 31 as the audience share for program "A". The share for program "B" would be

18.75 or 19. In the above example 1,600 represents the HUTS, or Homes Using Television out of the total TV households in the designated area. In this case HUTS = 57% (1,600/2,800).

CPM -Cost per thousand (not million!). When you are considering cost-effective ways of reaching potential customers it's important to be able to compare the media possibilities. To determine CPM you divide the cost of advertising by total number of people reached by the advertisement (in thousands). If a radio commercial costs $100 and reaches 50,000 people your CPM would be $2 (100/50,000). In the next module, we'll turn our attention to that important "blueprint" for the entire TV production, the script.

The Script — The Key Element in Productions

With the basic overview of the production process out of the way, we can look at the key element in the process: the script.

There are semi-scripted shows and fully scripted shows.

In the first category are interviews, discussions, ad-lib programs, and many demonstration and variety shows. These scripts resemble a basic outline, with only the segments and basic times listed.

Although scripts for a semi-scripted show may be comparatively easy to write (since there's very little to write!), this type of show puts pressure on the director and talent to figure things out as they go and to try to bring things together "on the fly."

Much in contrast, scripts for fully scripted shows list the complete audio and video for every minute. In a fully scripted show, the overall content, balance, pace, and timing can be figured out before the production starts in order to minimize unpleasant surprises.

The Concrete-to-Abstract Continuum

Documentary and hard news pieces should be reasonably concrete. That is, they should present information clearly, minimizing the possibility for misunderstanding.

In fact, the better you are at clearly explaining things, the more successful you'll be.

A concrete news script is quite different in approach and structure from the script for a feature story, soft news piece, music video, or dramatic production. In the latter cases, it's often desirable not to be too concrete — in order to allow room for personal interpretation.

Let's Look at Two Examples

An instructional video on the operation of a software program should be as explicit as possible. Given the nature of computers and computer programs, you should present information in a clear, systematic fashion.

Although you'll want to present the material in a creative, interesting, and possibly even humorous way, the challenge is in having all audience members acquire the same clear idea of a specific sequence of operational procedures. If most of the audience can successfully operate the program afterward, you're successful; if they can't, you're not. In contrast to this concrete type of production are feature pieces on Jazzercise or new fashions.

Given the fact that the audience has undoubtedly seen scores of television segments on fashion, the first challenge is to approach the segment in a fresh, creative, attention-getting way.

Compared to this challenge, presenting the piece is easy.

Unlike software programs or stereo components, fashions are not sold based on technical specifications. Because they appeal largely to the ego and emotions, we're less interested in communicating facts than in generating excitement, i.e., creating a positive emotional response.

Likewise, a soft news piece on exercise should not emphasize facts as much as action. Its approach should be more abstract. Instead of facts, its purpose is to communicate something of the feelings surrounding exercise and those that go along with having a slim, trim, fit body.

Hold their Interest

Once you establish the intent and focus of the production and you know the characteristics of the audience, you can select and arrange the program elements.

In scripting content, a logical and linear sequence is the most natural approach, especially when information must be presented in a precise, step-by-step fashion. Recall the instructional computer piece we cited.

Often, however, it's not desirable to use a structured, linear presentation. In fact, the latter can get a bit predictable and boring.

In dramatic productions, the techniques of using flashbacks (momentarily cutting back to earlier events) or presenting parallel stories (two or more stories running at the same time) can add variety and stimulate interest.

Whatever you do, be certain to present the materials in a way that will hold the attention and interest of your audience. You can do this by:

- engaging the audience's emotions
- presenting your ideas in fresh, succinct, clear, and creative ways
- making your viewers care about the subject matter
- using aural and visual variety.

While visualizing your scenes, if you discover spots that don't seem as if they would hold viewer attention, make changes.

Remember, if you lose your audience, you've compromised the whole purpose of your effort.

Spicing up Interviews

For better or worse, interviews serve as the mainstay of many, if not most, nondramatic productions. Because of this and the difficulty involved in making interviews interesting, they require special attention. (Later, we'll talk about interviewing techniques.)

Even though "talking heads" can get pretty boring, the credibility of an authority or the authenticity of the person directly involved in the story is generally better than a narrator presenting the same information.

However, except for rather intense and emotional subject matter, keep in mind that once we see what someone looks like during an interview, we will probably want to enhance interest and pace in our piece during the editing phase by cutting in B-roll (related supplementary) footage.

B-roll footage consists of shots of people, objects or places referred to in the basic interview footage — the A-roll.

At the same time, don't let the B-roll footage distract from what's being said. In television, "A-rolls" and B-rolls" refer to rolls or reels of videotape. At the same ime, other recording media are now replacing videotape. Although audio and video echnology changes rapidly, in this case and many others we tend to stick to the riginal (and often outdated) terms to describe things. Recall that in England, the TV ontrol room is still "the gallery" — a setting that hasn't been used since about 1940.

Whenever you plan an interview, plan for supplemental, B-roll footage. Sometimes you won't know what this will be until after the interview, so you need to keep your production options open.

In postproduction, you'll need to specify exact points in the interview (the A-roll) where the B-roll footage will go. Simply trying to describe points in scenes for edits can be difficult open the door to errors, not to mention require a lot of words. The only way to specify precise audio and video edit points is to use time-code numbers.

Time code, sometimes called SMPTE/EBU time code after the organizations that adopted it, refers to the eight-digit numbers that identify the exact hours, minutes, seconds, and frames in a video.

These numbers specify points on video recordings within at least 1/30th of a second — a level of accuracy important for a tightly edited show.

Assembling the Segments

Documentary writers who prefer a systematic approach (and have the luxury of time) start by typing — or having typed— a transcript of the interviews on a computer, complete with time-code references. This is especially valuable if they need to break up numerous lengthy interviews and rearrange them in a topical sequence.

Once on computer disk, writers can do word or phrase searches and quickly locate key words or topics in the interview segments.

Most word processing programs allow two or more windows on the screen.

Using this approach you can search and review the interview transcript in one window while writing the script in the other. Thus, you can easily condense, rearrange, and assemble the segments directly on the computer screen to provide the most logical and interesting flow.

If time-code numbers are included with the video segments, you should make a note of the time codes on the script as you go along, in case you later need to change anything.

In some instances you may be able to "run" video and audio sequences on the computer and see the results as you proceed.

Whenever it's necessary to explain or amplify points or establish bridges between interview segments, you can write narration. An announcer will generally read this over B-roll footage.

In writing the script, be alert at every moment to use the most effective means of getting your ideas across.

Ask yourself which technique(s) will best illustrate your point: narration, a short clip from an interview, an electronically animated sequence, a graph, or a still photo?

Some sophisticated editing programs have speech recognition capabilities, which means they can can search for spoken words or phrases in video footage.

As you pull the elements together, think of yourself as watching the show; try to visualize exactly what's going on at each moment. Great composers can hear each instrument in their heads as they write music. In the same way, effective scriptwriters visualize scenes as they write their scripts.

In establishing the pace of the production, eliminate long, slow periods and even long fast-moving periods. Either will tire an audience.

Except for a short, fast-paced montage (a rapid succession of images), keep shots segments to at least two seconds in length. Conversely, only a scene with plenty of action or intensity will be able to hold an audience for more than a minute.

Remember, engage your audience quickly and leave them with a positive impression at the end. In between, keep interest from drifting by varying pace, emotional content, and presentation style.

Scriptwriting Guidelines

Can a contractor build an office building without being able to understand the architect's blueprints? Not likely.

In the same way, key production personnel must understand the basics of scripts before they can create a production.

A comprehensive guide to scriptwriting is beyond the scope of this course. However, when you complete this module, you should understand the basic elements of scripts and even have a good start on writing one. (Remember: the most travelled route to producing is through writing.)

"Excuse Me, Mr. Brinkley..."

Many years ago, while dining in a Miami restaurant, a TV production student of mine saw David Brinkley, one of the most experienced and respected network anchorpersons of all time.* The student strode boldly up to Mr. Brinkley, introduced himself as an aspiring TV journalist, and asked:

"Mr. Brinkley, what advice could you give me to be successful in broadcast journalism?"

David Brinkley, who won more awards in news than any radio or TV newscaster in history, put down his fork, thought for a moment, and said, "Three things: Learn to write. Learn to write. And learn to write."

Although you can learn the basics of writing here or in a good book, you can become a good writer only by writing.

In a sense, initial failures aren't failures at all; they're a prerequisite for success. Thomas Edison said, "Genius is one percent inspiration and ninety-nine percent perspiration."

By another definition, *a genius* is a talented person who has done all his or her homework. These modules constitute the prerequisite homework involved in success.

Keep in mind that writing for the electronic media is not the same as writing for print. Those who write for print enjoy some advantages their broadcast counterparts don't have.

For example, a reader can go back and reread a sentence. If a sentence isn't understood in a TV production, however, the meaning is lost — or worse, the listener is distracted while figuring out what was said. With the written word, such things as chapter divisions, paragraphs, subheadings, italics, and boldface type guide the reader. And the spelling of sound-alike words can indicate their meaning.

Things are different when you write for the ear.

In order to deliver narration in a conversational style, you don't always follow standard rules of punctuation. Ellipses...three dots...are commonly used to designate pauses. Often, complete sentences aren't used...just as they aren't used in normal conversation. In broadcast writing an extra helping of commas provides clues to phrasing.

Although such usage is sometimes inconsistent with proper written form and your English 101 teacher may not approve, the overriding consideration in writing narration is *clarity*. This entails making it easy for an announcer to read, and making it easy for an audience to understand. The way we perceive verbal information also complicates things.

When we read, we see words in groups or thought patterns. This helps us grasp the meaning.

But, when we listen, information is delivered one word at a time.

To make sense out of a sentence we must retain the first words in memory while adding all subsequent words to them, until the sentence or thought is complete.

If the sentence is too complex or takes too long to unfold, meaning is missed or confused.

Of course, through proper phrasing and word emphasis a narrator can go a long way toward ensuring understanding. This gives the spoken word a major advantage over the written word.

Broadcast Style

Writers write video scripts in broadcast style. With allowance for sentence variety, video scripts use short, concise, direct sentences — weeding out unnecessary words.

You should also be aware of some common mistakes, such as the difference between *further* and *farther* and *less than* and *fewer than.*

Of course, the English language is constantly changing. Things which were deemed "wrong" at one point can eventually come into regular use and become accepted.

"Close proximity" is becoming accepted, even though *proximity* means *close,* so it's actually redundant.

"There are less concerns about good grammar in advertising" should be "fewer concerns." Fewer relates to things you can count; less to things you can't.

"Whom," even when correctly used in speech, now sounds stilted. "Irregardless" can be found in a couple of dictionaries—even though it's not seen as *acceptable*.

In writing your scripts, remember that the active voice is preferred over the inactive or passive voice. Nouns and verbs are preferred over adjectives, and specific words over general ones. Facts must be taut, verbs strong and active; a script should crackle.

Avoid dependent clauses at the beginning of sentences. Attribution should come at the beginning of sentences ("According to the Surgeon General...") rather than at the end, which is common in newspaper writing. In broadcast style, we want to know from the beginning who's doing the "saying."

The classic reference on writing clarity and simplicity is a little 70-page book called Elements of Style. Even many seasoned journalists keep it handy.

A recent book on punctuation is Lynne Truss' and Bonnie Timmons' *Eats, Shoots & Leaves.* Who would believe an instructional book on a mundane subject like *punctuation* could make the *New York Times* best-seller list? But as the saying goes, "It's not what you say, but how you say it" — something that's especially important in writing scripts.

Ten Newswriting Guidelines

With a bit of help from Ms. Debrah Potter of RTNDF, the Radio and Television News Directors Foundation, here are ten guidelines for writing news:

1. While making sure you bring the most interesting and surprising elements to the forefront of your story, don't give away everything right at the beginning. Maintain interest by spreading these "nuggets" throughout the story. And try not to let the lead-in to the story steal the thunder from what follows.
2. Use the active voice: subject, verb, and object.
3. Remember that nouns and verbs are stronger than adjectives and adverbs. Don't tell viewers what they should be feeling by using adjectives, especially shopworn adjectives, such as "tragic," "amazing," and "stunning." If the story's facts don't make such things obvious, you might want to examine your approach.
4. Avoid jargon; use well-known terms. For example, your audience probably won't know what *ENG* and *B-roll* mean.

5. Include defining details, such as the make of the car and the type of trees being cut down.
6. Write (tell!) the story as if you were trying to catch the interest of a friend. Try mentally to follow up on the phrases, "Guess what...," or "This may be hard to believe, but...."
7. After you write something, set it aside for at least ten minutes and concentrate on something else. Then go back and review the story with a fresh perspective.
8. Read the story aloud (not under your breath).

Rewrite

- sentences that are too long
- tongue-twisting or awkward phrases
- phrases that could be taken two ways
- long titles ("The 18-year-old, College Park Central High School sophomore...")

Don't rely on the sound track to tell the story or explain the video. The basic idea should be obvious from the video. At the same time, the audio and video should complement and strengthen each other. Screen the complete audio and video story (package) as a "doubting Thomas." Have you made statements that could legitimately be challenged? Your clearly stated and verified facts should silence any rational critic.

Correlate Audio and Video

Keep in mind the basic guideline of correlating (relating) audio and video because viewers are accustomed to having what they see on the screen relate to what they hear — generally in the form of dialogue or narration.

Even though you want audio and video to relate, watch out for the "see Dick run" approach where the audio states the obvious. If you can clearly see what's happening on the screen, this can get downright annoying.

Although radio drama had to slip many things into the dialogue to tip off the listeners to what they couldn't see ("Emma, why are you staring out the window?"), this is hardly the case with TV, where you can see what's taking place. The trick is to write slightly off the pictures. This means that, while you don't describe the pictures, your words aren't so far removed from what is being seen that you split viewer attention. This technique involves a delicate balancing act.

Information Overload

With more than one hundred TV channels available to viewers in some areas and millions of pages of information available on the Internet, to name just two sources of information, one of today's biggest problems is information overload.

In TV production the goal is not just to unload information on viewers. To be successful you must engage your audience and clearly communicate selected information in a manner that will both enlighten and possibly even entertain.

We can absorb only a limited amount of information at a time. The average viewer has preconceptions and internal and external distractions that get in the way.

If a script is packed with too many facts, or if the information is not clearly presented, the viewer will become confused, lost, and frustrated.

Lost vs. Bored

Not only is the amount of information you communicate important, but also the rate at which it's presented. In information-centered productions, give the viewer a chance to process each idea before moving on to the next.

If you move too rapidly, you'll lose your audience; too slowly, and you'll bore them.

The best approach in presenting crucial information in an instructional production is first to signal the viewer that something important is coming. Next, present the information as simply and clearly as possible.

Then, reinforce may points by repeating them in a different way — or with an illustration or two.

Here are seven general rules to remember in writing for television. Some of these apply to instructional productions, some to dramatic productions, and some to both.

- Assume a conversational tone by using short sentences and an informal, approachable style.
- Engage your audience emotionally; make them care about both the people and content of your production.
- Provide adequate logical structure; let viewers know where you're going, which concepts are key, and when you're going to change the subject.
- After making an important point, expound on it; illustrate it.
- 't try to pack too many facts into one program.
- Give your audience a chance to digest one concept before jumping to another.
- Pace your presentation according to the ability of your target audience to grasp the concepts.

Video Grammar

Some people say that, unlike writing, video and film production don't have standardized grammar (e.g., conventions or structure).

Although video has abandoned much of the grammar established by early filmmaking, even in this MTV, YouTube era we can use various techniques to add structure to formal productions.

In dramatic productions, lap-dissolves (when two video sources overlap for a few seconds during the transition from one to the other) often signal a change in time or place.

Fade-ins and fade-outs, which apply to both audio and video, can be likened to the beginning and end of book chapters. A fade-out consists of a two-or three-second transition from a full signal to black and silence. A fade-in is the reverse.

Fade-ins and fade-outs often signal a major change or division in a production, such as a major passage of time. (But "often" is a long way from "always.") Traditionally, teleplays (television plays) and screenplays (film scripts) start with a fade-in and close with a fade-out.

Although we don't focus on dramatic film scripts here, one film writer-producer told us about a saying he has taped over his desk: *'It's the story, stupid.'*

Script Terms and Abbreviations

A number of terms and abbreviations are used in scriptwriting. Some describe camera movements. When the entire camera is moved toward or away from the subject, it's referred to as a dolly.

A zoom, an optical version of a dolly, achieves somewhat the same effect. A script notation might say, "Camera zooms in for close-up of John" or "Camera zooms out to show John is not alone."

A lateral move is a truck.

Some Terms Designate Shots.

Cuts or takes are instant transitions from one video source to another. In grammatical terms, shots can be likened to sentences where each shot is a visual statement.

The cover shot or establishing shot are designated on a script by "wide-shot" (WS) or "long shot" (LS). Occasionally, the abbreviations XLS for extreme long shot or VLS for very long shot are used. These all can give the audience a basic orientation to the geography of a scene (i.e., who is standing where) after which you'll cut to closer shots.

In the relatively low-resolution medium of standard-definition television (SDTV), this type of shot is visually weak because important details aren't easy to see. Film and HDTV (high-definition television) don't have quite the same problem.

Cover or establishing shots should be held only long enough to orient viewers to the relationship between major scene elements. (How close is the burning shed to the house?) Thereafter, they can be momentarily used as reminders or updates on scene changes as reestablishing shots.

TV scripts are usually divided into audio and video columns, with shot designations in the left video column.

Costing out A Production

Unfortunately, the best things in life are not always free. This applies especially to major television shows, which can cost millions of dollars an hour to produce. Although you may have come up with a truly great idea for a script — one you're certain will make you famous! — unless you can raise the money to get it produced it'll remain simply that: a great idea. So the first question is what will it cost to produce?

Even if you have no interest in producing, the better your grasp of this issue, the better your chance of success. And keep in mind that no production company will commit to a production without a reasonable idea of how much it will cost. We call this process costing out a production.

Traditionally, we think of expenses as falling into two broad areas: above-the-line and below-the-line.

Above-the-Line and Below-the-Line

Although the "line" blurs at times, above-the-line expenses generally relate to the performing and producing elements: talent, script, music, and others.

Below-the-line elements refer to two broad areas:

- the physical elements: sets, props, make-up, wardrobe, graphics, transportation, production equipment, studio facilities, and editing
- the technical personnel: stage manager, engineering personnel, video recording operators, audio operators, and general labour

To cost out a major production accurately, you can go beyond the above-the-line and below-the-line designations and divide production into at least 15 categories:

1. preproduction costs
2. location scouting and related travel expenses

3. studio rental
4. sets and set construction
5. on-location expenses
6. equipment rental
7. video recording and duplication
8. production crew costs
9. producer, director, writer, creative fees
10. on-camera talent costs
11. insurance, shooting permits, contingencies, etc.
12. on-line and off-line editing
13. advertising, promotion, and publicity
14. research and follow-up
15. materials, supplies, and miscellaneous expenses

Smaller productions, of course, will not involve all of these categories.

You can list these categories and their projected costs in a column on the left side of a computer spreadsheet program, such as Microsoft Excel.

You can then add corresponding formulas that will later automatically generate totals. You'll then be able to adjust expenses as needed during the production and immediately see the effect on the bottom line.

Renting vs. Buying Equipment

Note that one of the categories covers equipment rental. Except for studio equipment that's used every day, it's often more economical to rent equipment rather than buy it.

First, *production equipment — especially cameras and recorders — becomes outdated quickly.* At more than $70,000 for a top-notch video camera, you might assume you'll recoup the cost through several years' use. If you pay cash for a $70,000 camera and use it five years, the cost breaks down to $14,000 a year, plus repair and maintenance expenses.

Even though the camera might still be reliable after five years or more, compared to the newer models it will be outdated. It may even be difficult to find parts.

Several different production facilities can use equipment available for rent, however. This means the rental company can write off the initial investment on their taxes more quickly, making it possible to replace the equipment with newer models.

Even for consumer grade equipment, the rental cost (which may be only $50 a day) might make sense if you'll use it for just a few days.

Second, the rental company, rather than the production facility, is responsible for repair, maintenance, and updating. If equipment breaks down during a shoot (production), rental companies will typically replace it within a few hours.

Third, renting provides an income tax advantage. When equipment is purchased, it must be depreciated (written off on income tax) over a number of years. But sometimes this time span exceeds the practical usefulness of the equipment. This may mean that the production facility will need to sell the used equipment in order to recoup some of their initial investment. (Companies often donate their equipment to schools for a tax write-off.) If you rent non-studio equipment, however, you can write it off immediately as a production expense.

Although rules governing income taxes change regularly, deducting the cost of rental equipment can represent a quicker, simpler — and in many cases greater — tax deduction.

Finally, when you rent equipment, you increase the opportunities to obtain equipment that will meet the specific needs of your production. Purchasing equipment can generate pressure to use it, even though at times other makes and models might be better suited to your needs.

Approaches to Attributing Costs

Once you figure out the cost of a production, you may need to justify it, either in terms of cost-effectiveness or expected results.

There are three bases on which to measure cost effectiveness:

- cost per minute
- cost per viewer
- cost vs. measured benefits.

Cost Per Minute

Cost per minute is relatively easy to determine; simply divide the final production cost by the duration of the finished product. For example, if a 30-minute production costs $120,000, the cost per minute is $4,000.

Cost Per Viewer

Cost per viewer is also relatively simple to figure out; divide the total production cost by the actual or anticipated audience.

In the field of advertising, CPM (or cost-per-*thousand*) is a common measure. If 100,000 people see a show that costs $5,000 to produce, the CPM is $50. On a cost-per-viewer basis, this comes out to be only five cents a person.

Cost Per Measured Results

Cost per measured results is the most difficult to determine. Here, we must measure production costs against intended results.

Suppose that after airing one 60-second commercial we'll sell 300,000 packages of razor blades at a resulting profit of $100,000. If we spent a million dollars producing and airing the commercial, we would have to question whether it was good investment.

But, advertisers air most ads more than once. (Sometimes endlessly, it seems!) If the cost of TV time is $10,000 and we sell 300,000 packages of razor blades after each airing, we will soon show a profit.

All of these "measured results" are easily determined by a calculator.

Return on Investment

What if we also run ads in newspapers and on radio, and we have huge, colorful displays in stores? Then it becomes difficult to determine the cost-effectiveness of each medium, and the question becomes, which approaches are paying off and which aren't?

And there can be another issue. We can count razor blades, but it may be more difficult to determine the returns on other "products."

For example, it's very difficult to determine the effectiveness of programming on altering human behaviour and attitudes.

How do you quantify the return on investment of public service announcements designed to get viewers to stop smoking, "buckle up for safety," or preserve clean air and water?

Even if we conduct before-and-after surveys to measure changes in public awareness, it can be almost impossible to factor out the influence of the host of other voices the public may encounter on that issue.

Apart from in-depth interviews with viewers, we may have to rely largely on "the record."

If we know a series of 60-second TV spots increases razor blade sales by 300,000, we might assume a 60-second PSA would also have some influence on smoking, buckling seat belts, and preserving clean air and water. The question is how many people modified their behaviour as *a direct result* of your PSA?

This is important for nonprofits and other organizations to know in order to determine the best use of their informational and educational dollars.

How the Imaging Process Works

Why do you need to know how the film and TV imaging process works?

For one thing, knowledge is power, and the more you know about the process, the easier it will be to use the tools creatively.

Plus, you'll be able to solve most of the inevitable problems that crop up during TV production.

Fields and Frames

Ironically, both "motion" pictures and TV are based solidly on an illusion. "Motion" as such does not exist in the actual TV and motion picture images. The illusion is created when a rapid sequence of still images are presented.

This illusion was discovered after a $25,000 bet was established by a motion picture foundation in 1877. For decades, an argument raged over whether a race horse ever had all four hooves off the ground at the same time.

By the way, the horse in the above illustration should be in motion. If it isn't, you may need to turn on the animation in your browser in order to see this and other animated illustrations in these modules.

In an effort to settle the issue Leland Stanford, founder of Stanford University, set up an experiment in which a photographer took a rapid sequence of photos of a running horse. (And, yes, they found that for brief moments a race horse does have all four feet off the ground at the same time.)

However, this experiment established something even more important. It illustrated that, if a sequence of still pictures is presented at a rate of about 16 or more per-second, the individual pictures blend together and give the impression of a continuous, uninterrupted image.

If the series of eleven still photos shown below are presented sequentially in rapid succession, they create the appearance of continuous motion.

You can see in the sequence of images above that the individual pictures vary slightly to reflect changes over time.

In the circular illustration on the right we've slowed down the timing of the images. Here, you can see more clearly how a sequence of still images can create an illusion of movement.

We see a more primitive version of this in the "moving" lights of a theatre marquee or "moving" arrow of a neon sign suggesting passersby come in and buy something. Although early silent films used basic frame (picture) rates of 16 and 18 per second, when sound was introduced the rate increased to 24 frames per-second.

This was necessary primarily to meet the quality needs of the sound track. (Actually, to reduce flicker, today's motion picture projectors use a two-bladed shutter that projects each frame twice, giving an effective rate of 48 frames per-second.)

For decades, film has maintained a worldwide 24 frame-per-second sound standard, unlike broadcast television with frame rates of 25 and 30 per-second, depending on the country.

The NTSC (National Television System Committee) system of television used in the United States, Canada, Japan, Mexico, and a few other countries reproduces pictures (frames) at a rate of approximately 30 per-second.

Of course, this presents a bit of a problem in converting film to TV (mathematically, 24 doesn't go into 30 very well), but we'll worry about that later. A motion picture camera records a completely formed still picture on each frame of film, just like the still pictures on a roll of film in a 35mm camera. It's just that the motion picture camera takes the individual pictures at a rate of 24 per-second.

Things are different in TV. In a video camera, hundreds of horizontal lines make up each frame.

Thousands of points of brightness and colour information exist along each of these lines. This information is electronically discerned in the TV camera and then reproduced on a TV display in a left-to-right, top-to-bottom scanning sequence. This sequence is similar to the movement of your eyes as you read.

Interlaced Scanning

Originally, to reduce variations in flicker and brightness during the scanning process, as well as to solve some technical limitations, the scanning process was divided into two halves.

The odd-numbered lines were scanned first and then the even-numbered lines were interleaved between these lines to create a complete picture. Not surprisingly, we refer to this process as interleaved or interlaced scanning.

In this greatly enlarged TV image, we've coloured the odd lines green and the even lines yellow. When we remove these colours, we can see how they combine to create the black and white video picture on the right. (Later, we'll describe a colour TV picture, which is a bit more complex.) Each of these half-frame passes (either all of the odd-or all of the even-numbered lines, or the green or the yellow lines in the illustration) is a field. The completed (two-field) picture is a frame. After scanning the complete picture (frame), the process starts again. But, if the subject matter in the scene changes with time, the next frame will reflect that slight change. Human perception fuses together these slight changes between successive pictures, giving the illusion of continuous, uninterrupted motion.

The interleaved approach, although necessary before recent advances in technology, results in minor picture "artifacts," or distortions in the picture, including variations in colour.

Progressive Scanning

After several decades of using the interlaced approach, today more and more video systems (including computer monitors and new flat-screen TV sets) use a progressive or non-interlaced scanning approach. With this approach, the fields (odd and even lines) are combined and reproduced together in a 1-2-3 sequence, rather than an odd (1-3-5) and even (2-4-6) interlaced sequence.

Progressive scanning has a number of advantages, including greater clarity and the ability to interface more easily with computer-based video equipment. But it adds greater technical demands on the TV system. As we'll see in the next module, the specifications for digital and high-definition television (DTV, HDTV) allow for both progressive and interlaced scanning.

The Camera's Imaging Device

The lens of the television camera forms an image on a light sensitive target inside a video camera in the same way a motion picture camera forms an image on film.

But instead of film, television cameras commonly use a solid-state, light-sensitive receptor called a CCD (charged-coupled device) or, more commonly, a CMOS (complementary metal oxide semiconductor). Both of these "chips" are able to detect brightness differences at different points throughout the image area.

The chip's *target area* (the small rectangular area near the centre of this photo) contains from hundreds-of-thousands to millions of pixel (picture element) points. Each point can electrically respond to the amount of light focused on its surface.

A very small section of a chip is represented below — enlarged thousands of times. The individual pixels are shown in blue. Differences in image brightness detected at each of these points on the surface of the chip change that light into electric voltages.

Electronics within the camera scanning system regularly check each pixel area to determine the amount of light falling on its surface.

This sequential information is directed to an output amplifier along the path shown by the red arrows.

This information readout results in constantly changing field and frame information.

In a sense, your TV receiver reverses this process.

The pixel-point voltages generated in a camera are changed back into light, which we see as an image on our TV screens.

Analog and Digital Signals

Electronic signals — as they originate in microphones and cameras— are analog (or analogue) in form. This means the equipment detects signals in terms of continuing variations in relative strength or amplitude. In audio, this translates into volume or *loudness*; in video, it's the *brightness* of the picture.

As illustrated above, we can change these analog signals (on the left) into *digital data* (on the right). The latter is computer zeros and ones (0s and 1s, or binary computer code). The digital signal is then sent to subsequent electronic equipment. Backing up a bit, we need to explain how the analog-to-digital process works. The top part of the illustration below shows how an analog signal can rise and fall over time to reflect changes in the original audio or video source.

In order to change an analog signal to digital, that wave pattern is sampled at a high rate of speed. The amplitude at each of those sampled moments (shown in blue-green on the left) is converted into a number equivalent.

These numbers are simply the combinations of the 0s and 1s used in computer language.

Since we are dealing with numerical quantities, this conversion process is appropriately called quantizing.

Once the information is converted into numbers, we can do some interesting things (generally, special effects) by adding, subtracting, multiplying, and dividing the numbers.

The faster all this is done, the better the audio and video quality. But this means that as the quality increases the technical requirements become more demanding.

Thus, we are frequently dealing with the difference between high-quality equipment that can handle ultra high-speed data rates and lower-level (less expensive) consumer equipment that relies on a reduced sampling rate. This, in part, answers the question about why some video recorders cost $300 and others cost $100,000.

What's the Advantage of Digital Data?

Compared to the digital signal, an analog signal would seem to be the most accurate and ideal representation of the original signal. While this may initially be true, the problem arises in the need for constant amplification and re-amplification of the signal throughout every stage of the audio and video process.

Whenever an analog signal is reproduced or amplified noise is inevitably introduced, which degrades the signal.

In audio, this can take the form of a hissing sound; in video, it appears as a subtle background "snow" effect.

By converting the original analog signal into digital form, we can eliminate this noise buildup, even though the signal is amplified or "copied" dozens of times.

Because digital signals are limited to the form of 0s and 1s, no "in-between" information (spurious noise) can creep in to degrade the signal.

We'll delve more deeply into some of these issues when we focus on digital audio.

Today's digital audio and video equipment has borrowed heavily from developments in computer technology — so heavily, in fact, that the two areas are now merging.

Satellite services such as DISH and Direct TV make use of digital receivers that are, in effect, specialized computers. Progressive radio and TV stations have already switched from analog to digital signal processing. And you probably listen to music recorded on a pocket-sized device capable of storing several hours of digitized music.

The Move to Digital

The move to digital video and audio has had a major impact on the entire production and postproduction process.

- Suddenly, your desktop or laptop computer can be turned into a videotape-editing console. (Complete, 90-minute productions — even feature-length films — are now being edited on PCs and laptop computers.)
- New three-chip DVCPro camcorders can equal the quality of the MII and Betacam analog formats-formerly the high-quality standards in video field production.
- The terms off line and on line editing may soon be obsolete distinctions.

Although digital signal processing has changed many areas of audio and video, we'll talk about just one area here: digital video recording. Since the digital signal is recorded in terms of clearly defined "off" and "on" (or "0" and "1") pulses just the way computer information is, there is no generational loss in making digital copies.

A fifth generation recording from the best analog VTR shows signs of deterioration. A fifth, or even the 50th generation of digital video is not significantly different from the original. This advantage is extremely important in postproduction, where video may have to go through multiple generations of special effects.

Next, the signal-to-noise ratio of digital video remains consistent through repeated stages of amplification and signal processing. (The signal-to-noise ratio is the degree to which video or audio information stands out from background interference, or noise. The higher the signal-to-noise ratio, the clearer and stronger the signal will be.)

Because sophisticated error correction equipment is normally a part of digital equipment, playbacks are immune to most video problems. These include dropouts, velocity errors, impact errors, and general colour errors.

Next, digital video can be processed by computer equipment without going through analog-to-digital conversion.

And finally, digital videotapes have a much better "shelf life" than analog tapes, which means they are better suited for storage and archival use.

U.S. DTV Standards

The simplified chart below outlines the various Advanced Television Systems Committee digital standards adopted in the United States.

Although there are numerous factors involved in evaluating technical quality, from a purely technical standpoint the greater number of scan lines on the screen at any one time the clearer the picture will be. In addition, the progressive approach to scanning will result in a higher technical quality than the interlaced approach.

It should be noted that the HDTV standard of 1,080 lines shown below is the same as previously discussed the 1,125-line HDTV standard. The difference centres on the total lines broadcast (1,125) vs. the active visible lines (1,080). As in

SDTV, many of the lines that are broadcast do not end up being displayed on the TV screen.

Active Lines Per Picture	*Pixels Per Line*	*Aspect Ratio*	*Frame Rate*	*Scanning Approach*
1080	1920	16:9	24, 30, and 60	Progressive
1080	1920	16:9	24, 30, and 60	Interlaced
720	1280	16:9	24, 30, and 60	Progressive
720	704	16:9	24, 30, and 60	Interlaced
480	640	4:3, 16:9	24, 30, and 60	Progressive
480	640	4:3	24, 30, and 60	Interlaced

To simplify things some minor formats are not listed.

720p vs. 1080i

There are ongoing debates on whether 1080i or 720p is better for HDTV.

Those who say 1080i is better say that 2,073,600 pixels for HDTV are "clearly" superior to the 921,600 used in 720p. The more lines, the more picture detail.

But, again, there's the issue of the number of lines that appear at one time. Since 720 is progressive and 1080i isn't. This means that the 720 standard ends up being better for tracking action, plus you won't see any "jaggies" or motion artifacts with 720p. The newest tuners or analog-to-digital TV converters can convert any of these standards into a TV receiver display. At the same time, some tuners/receivers display one standard better than another.

The 24p Standard

So-called e-cinema or digital cinema has moving to the 24p standard (24 frames per-second, progressive scan). Those who are after the "film look" prefer 24p, because the progressive approach results in fewer artifacts (aberrations) and because the 24 fps video rate is the same as film.

When projected, and with the proper equipment and electronic setup, both 24p and full HDTV become almost indistinguishable from film. If there is any "fault" with digital video it's that seems "too sharp and clear" compared to film.

Part I

World Television Standards and DTV/HDTV

Fifty years ago it didn't matter much that there were a dozen or so incompatible systems of television in the world. Distance was a great insulator.

But times have changed. Today, satellites link every country with television, and the Internet provides video, audio, and the written word to virtually anyone anywhere who has a computer and telephone line.

Now, incompatible broadcast standards, not to mention scores of different languages, represent a barrièr to communication and understanding.

Dictators like it that way, as do others who fear that the free flow of information will undermine their views and threaten their control.

This is why many countries spend millions of dollars each year to keep out undesirable information. (An example that few people in the United States know about is the *jamming* that has taken place on international short wave. This is discussed here.) Recall that we previously discussed the meaning of the coloured boxes before these links.

Most of the rest of us — especially those who live in democracies — feel a free flow of information is essential not only to progress, but also to dissolve barriers of misunderstanding between peoples. Films, TV, and the Internet— and especially e-mail between individuals in different countries — all show that, despite conflicting politics and religions, people the worldover have pretty much the same hopes, fears, and dreams. Touching on these basic human similarities is a major goal of TV production.

International program distribution is essential to financial success. Films and TV programs represent two of the major exports of the United States. In fact, many productions don't begin to show a profit until they go into international distribution.

In addition to the problems related to a free flow of ideas and information we must confront technical incompatibilities among broadcast systems.

This means a program produced in one country can't automatically be viewed in many other countries without converting it to a different technical standard. These technical differences relate to both to incompatibilities in equipment and in the approach to broadcasting the audio and video signals.

Some 14 different TV broadcast standards have been used at different times throughout the world. Excluding DTV (digital TV), today the following three basic systems serve the vast majority of countries, although some significant incompatibilities exist within some of them:

- NTSC (National Television System Committee)
- SECAM (Sequential Colour and Memory)
- PAL (Phase Alternating Line).

Within these there are four major differences:

- the total number of horizontal lines in the picture (525 or 625 for standard-definition TV (SDTV) and 1,125 and 1,250 for high-definition TV (HDTV)
- whether the transmission rate is 25 or 30 frames (complete pictures) per-second
- the broadcast channel width (data bandwidth of the signal)
- whether an AM or FM signal is used for transmitting audio and video.

Historically, the number of lines used in standard broadcast TV has ranged from the United Kingdom's 405-line system to France's 819-line system. The phase-out of both these systems has left us with the 525 and 625 standards for SDTV (Standard-Definition TV).

You might think this a bit technical, but hang in there. It's relevant to what you need to know. The quick matching game at the end of the chapter will tell how much of the chapter has sunk in.

Aspect Ratios

Although the number of scanning lines may have varied, until recently all television systems had a 4:3 aspect ratio. The aspect ratio is the width-height proportion of the picture.

The 4:3 ratio was consistent with motion pictures that predated the wide screen aspect ratios used in CinemaScope, VistaVision, and Panavision.

HDTV uses a 16:9 aspect ratio. In the picture here, the wider area represents HDTV. The most commonly used wide-screen movie formats are slightly larger than 16:9 (although the difference is insignificant). The CinemaScope film aspect ratio, however, is wider than 16:9.

The NTSC Broadcast Standard

The United States, Canada, Greenland, Mexico, Cuba, Panama, Japan, the Philippines, Puerto Rico, and most of South America share the National Television System Committee's (NTSC's) 525-line, 30 frames-per-second system.

The NTSC standard for black and white (monochrome) television was developed in 1941. By 1953, a colour standard had been finalized.

The NTSC's 60-field system originally based its timing cycle on the 60 Hz (hertz or cycle) electrical system these countries use. Since other countries in the world use a 50 Hz electrical system, they developed systems of television based on 50 fields per-second.

The basic NTSC standard is more than 50 years old, and many technical improvements came along during the subsequent half-century. Digital TV standards, which we'll cover later, take advantage of many new technical capabilities and provide major improvements over the original NTSC standard.

The PAL and SECAM Television Systems

More than half of all countries use one of two 625-line, 25-frame systems: SECAM (Sequential Colour and Memory) or PAL (Phase Alternating Line). France originally developed SECAM as a non-compatible system designed to protect their country's manufacturing industry from foreign electronic imports. Because SECAM is incompatible with other TV systems, Communist countries adopted it in part to prevent their people from seeing and being influenced by TV programming from noncommunist countries. Technically, SECAM is the simplest TV system.

PAL is a modified and somewhat improved version of NTSC. It was developed in Germany and is used in Britain and most of Western Europe. Except for Brazil, all PAL systems have 625 lines. The extra 100 lines in SECAM and most PAL systems add significant detail and clarity to the video picture, but the 50 fields per second (compared to 60 fields in the NTSC system) means the viewer can sometimes notice a slight flicker. Even so, the 25 frames-per-second (fps) standard is very close to the international film standard of 24 fps. Therefore, we can easily convert the 24-fps film standard to the PAL and SECAM video systems. (Slightly speeding up film to 25 fps is hard to notice.)

The Film and Video Conversion Processes

This takes a bit of fancy footwork, as explained here. This link also explains how we convert NTSC video to PAL and SECAM video and vice versa.

Digital and High-Definition Television

HDTV contains over two million individual pixels, resulting in pictures six to ten times sharper than SDTV. Although by early 2009 all TV stations in the U.S. should be digital, digital does not (necessarily) mean high definition. More on that as we go along.

High-Definition/Digital Television

The greater sharpness of HDTV is coupled with the wide-screen (16:9) images and Dolby Digital 5.1 surround-sound.

The table below compares the basic attributes of U.S. SDTV and HDTV television systems.

Note that, although we consider HDTV to have 1,125 lines, only 1,080 of these are "active" or visible on the screen.

Standards	*SDTV (Analog)*	*HDTV (Digital)*
Total Lines	525	1125
Active Lines	480-486 (maximum visible on the screen)	1080 (maximum visible on the screen)
Sound	Two channels (stereo)	5.1 channels (surround sound)
Max Resolution	720 X 486	1920 X 1080

According to the original timetable that the FCC (the Federal Communications Commission, the primary governing agency for U.S. broadcasting), by the year 2006 all SDTV television in the U.S. was to be phased out in favor of DTV (digital television). Of course, it didn't happen — primarily because things couldn't move that fast.

The FCC then moved that deadline to Feb. 17, 2009. However, because government funds for underwriting user decoder boxes could not meet demand, on January 26th the Senate approved a four-month delay in the digital TV conversion. However, just two days after the Senate unanimously passed the plan, House Republicans voted down the Senate move to delay the transition. But then on Feb. 4th the House reversed itself and approved a June 12th deadline.

When the switch to digital finally came on June 12th, more than 900 full-power TV stations permanently shut down their analog signals. Considering how major this transition was, things went relatively smoothly. Even so, millions of people still weren't ready and their TV screens went to snow or were simply blank. Although only stations being received by rabbit ears or rooftop antennas (and not by cable or satellite) were affected, a significant percent of the U.S. population discovered that all of their favourite TV programs "unexpectedly" disappeared. There were still there, of course, but now on digital frequencies. These frequencies, which for some people required a new antenna to reliably receive, allow for many additional services.

The Anatomy of Digital TV Signals

Unlike SDTV, which has only one broadcast standard in the United States, eighteen digital standard options exist within the new U.S. DTV/HDTV standards. Although it might seem these different approaches would represent technical chaos, TV tuners and signal converters are designed to automatically sort out the differences and deliver a standard signal to TV receivers.

DTV standards vary in Three Ways

- Active lines of resolution: 1,080 and 720 for HDTV; only 480 for SDTV.
- Types of scanning: Interlaced (two fields, each consisting of half the lines merge to make one complete frame or picture), and progressive (all lines transmitted together without interlacing). Recall we covered this concept here.
- Scan rate: 60 or 50 fields per-second for interlaced, 30 or 25 frames per second for progressive, and 24 frames per-second for film-style progressive scan.

We now commonly use 24 fps in high-definition video production — especially when a need exists to convert the results to film. Attack of the Clones, the Star Wars film release of 2002, was one of the first "films" done on 24-progressive video and then converted to film. Today, not only do almost all theatrical films produced depend to some degree on digital imaging, but many theatres now have digital (filmless) projection systems.

4

News Broadcasting

Here we consider what makes one thing worth reporting, while another thing is not. We offer a test for news which can work in all societies. We consider what makes some news stories stronger than others. Finally, we look at how news comes to journalists, and the areas of life where we most often find it. Life appears to be a shapeless jumble of events, falling over each other, elbowing and jostling each other.

Journalists each day structure this chaos, so that the public receives it sorted out and neatly packaged into stories, the same day on radio, television or online and the next day in newspapers. It will have been evaluated.

The biggest news will be given first in the bulletin or on Page One of the paper, in detail; lesser news will be given in less detail later in the bulletin or on an inside page; and the rubbish will have been thrown away. How do journalists decide what is news and what is not? How do they distinguish between a big news story and a small one? The answer is that they do it in exactly the same way as everybody else. Everybody makes those same judgments whenever they decide to talk about one event rather than another.

For example, which do you think is more interesting:

a) A girl going to primary school, to high school, or to university?

b) A man aged 25 marrying a girl aged 20, or a man aged 55 marrying a girl aged 15?

c) A car killing a chicken, a pig or a child?

Every one of these events might be news for the community in which it happens, but some are more newsworthy than others.

You very likely answered that the most interesting things were a girl going to university, a man aged 55 marrying a girl aged 15, and a car killing a child. If your answer was different, though, it does not necessarily mean that you were wrong.

The same event can have different levels of interest in different societies, and will be talked about in different ways. If a farm wall has collapsed, killing a cow and a pig, which is more important? Clearly, the answer will vary from one society to another, depending upon the relative importance of cows and pigs.

For this reason, the content of the news can be different in different societies. The way in which the news is judged, though, is the same everywhere.

Criteria of News

The criteria by which news is judged are:

- Is it new?
- Is it unusual?
- Is it interesting or significant?
- Is it about people?

Is it New?

If it is not new, it cannot be news. The assassination of Mrs Gandhi is unusual, interesting, significant and about people, but it cannot possibly be reported in tomorrow's papers, because it is not new.

If some facts about that assassination became known for the first time, however, that would be news. The assassination would not be new, but the information would be.

Events which happened days or even weeks earlier can still be news, as long as they have not been reported before. If you are telling a story for the first time, it is new to your readers or listeners and therefore it can be news. News of the death of Mao Tse-tung, for instance, was not released to the world by the Chinese government for several days; when they did release it, however, it was still very definitely news.

Is it Unusual?

Things are happening all the time, but not all of them are news, even when they are new. A man wakes up, eats breakfast and goes to work on a bus; it has only just happened, but nobody wants to read about it because it is not unusual. Ordinary and everyday things do not make news.

Of course, if that same man was 90 years old and was still catching the bus to work every day, it would be unusual!

The classic definition of news is this: "Dog bites man" is not news; "Man bites dog" is news.

This definition, though, is not universal. If dogs are eaten in your society (at feasts, for instance) then it will not be news when a man bites a dog-so long as it has been cooked.

What is usual in one society may be unusual in another. Again, we will expect the content of the news to vary from society to society. In every society, though, whatever is unusual is likely to be news.

Is it Interesting?

Events which are new and unusual may still not be of general interest. Scientists may report that an insect has just been found living on a plant which it did not previously inhabit. The discovery is new, and the event is unusual, but it is unlikely to interest anybody other than a specialist or enthusiast.

In a specialist publication this could be big news, but in a general news broadcast or paper it would merit at most a few words.

Is it Significant?

However, if that same insect was one which had a huge appetite, and which had previously lived on and eaten bush grass and if the new plant on which it had been found was rice, then the story becomes news, because it is significant.

People may not be interested in bugs, but they are interested in food. If this insect is now threatening their crops, it becomes a matter of concern to them. It is news because it is significant.

Similarly, if a peasant farmer says that the Roman Catholic Church should ordain women priests, that is not news. If an archbishop says it, it is news, because what he says on the subject is significant. It is the views of people such as the archbishop which help to form the policy of the Church.

Once again, what is interesting or significant in one society may not be interesting or significant in another. The content of the news may be different, therefore, in different societies, but the way it is identified will be the same.

Is it about People?

Most news is automatically about people, because it is the things people do to change the world which makes news.

However, news can also be made by non-human sources, such as a cyclone, a bush fire, a drought, a volcanic eruption or an earthquake. It is when reporting these stories that it is important to make sure that the story is centred on people.

The cyclone would not matter if it blew itself out in the middle of the Pacific Ocean, away from any inhabited islands; the fire could burn for as long as it likes in bush where nobody lives; the Sahara Desert has a near-permanent drought, but in most of it nobody is there to rely on rains; a volcanic eruption or an earthquake which damages nobody's property and injures nobody is really not news.

All these natural disasters only become news when they affect people's lives. Every story can be told in terms of people. Always start by asking yourself the question: "How does this affect my readers', listeners' or viewers' lives?"

Whenever you have a story which tells of how something has happened which affects both people and property, always put the people first

RIGHT: More than 100 people were left homeless after Cyclone Victor struck Suva yesterday.

WRONG: Seventeen houses were flattened when Cyclone Victor struck Suva yesterday.

How Strong a Story?

A story which is new, unusual, interesting, significant and about people is going to be a very good story indeed. One way of deciding the strength of a story is to check how many of those five criteria it meets.

There are other factors, though, which make stories strong or weak:

Closeness

The same event happening in two different places can have two quite different news values. A coup d'état in your own country is as big a story as you can ever have (although you will probably not be at liberty to report it as you would wish!). A coup in the country next door is still a big story, because it may affect the stability of your own country.

However, a coup in a small country in another continent is unlikely to merit more than a few paragraphs. The appeal of local news is that your readers or listeners might know the people or place involved.

Remember, though, that the word "local" means different things to different people. If you broadcast to a wide area or sell your newspaper in many different towns, you must realise that a small story which interests readers in one place, because it is local, may not be of any interest to readers elsewhere.

Personal Impact

The average reader, listener or viewer may be a parent, a person wanting a good education for the children, dreaming of buying a car, looking forward to going home on leave, anticipating the next big community feast or festival. You will need to have a very clear understanding of what your own readers or listeners are like.

So stories about bride-price or dowries, children, land disputes, new schools, cheaper or dearer fares, or whatever else is important and may affect your average reader, will have personal impact. People can identify with stories about other people like themselves. So those stories with which many people can identify are stronger than those which only apply to a few.

How do we get News?

A lot of news will come to you as a journalist without any real effort on your part. Government handouts, Ministers' speeches and announcements of new developments come into the newsroom after being processed by press officers or public relations officers. Passing on such information, as long as it is genuinely interesting and informative, is an important function of the media, to provide society with the hard facts of what is happening in the country.

It is part of your job as a journalist to sort out what is interesting and informative from the millions of boring words which may be sent to you. There is also news which journalists find for themselves and reveal to the public. This need not be a subject which somebody wants to be kept secret. Many people have a story to tell but do not know how to write a media release. It is part of your job as a journalist to find these people and report their stories.

There are also some stories which people want to keep secret but which the public ought to know about. When you hear about such a situation, it is your duty to investigate fairly but fearlessly.

Where does News come From?

Now we know what makes news: The following are the main areas of life in which we expect frequently to find news stories. For each category below, think of at least one event or situation which could make a news story in your own society.

Conflicts: This category includes wars, strikes, revolutions, secessionist groups, tribal and clan fights, elections and the power battles of politics.

Disaster and tragedy: This may include air crashes, train crashes, ships sinking, volcanic eruptions, earthquakes, or human tragedies like children falling down deep wells from which they cannot be rescued.

Progress and development: Development is always news in a developing country. The report should be always of how the changes affect people's lives, for better or for worse. New ideas or progress in one area may stimulate ideas in another. Development stories may include education, the development of new technology, improvement of farming techniques, road building and irrigation schemes. Citizens of more developed countries may also appreciate stories about developments in things which affect their lives or well-being, such as medical breakthroughs, new technologies or initiatives to make transport easier, quicker or cheaper.

Crime: Any crime can be news, whether it is a road traffic offence, break and enter, corruption, forgery, rape or murder-but more serious crimes or unusual crimes generally make bigger news stories.

Money: These stories include fortunes made and lost, school fees, taxes, the Budget, food prices, wage rises, economic crises and compensation claims.

It is not only large sums of money which make news; the little girl who gives her only ten cents to a huge fund-raising event is more interesting than the businessman who gives $100.

The underdog: This is one of the great themes of literature and drama (David and Goliath, the Hare and the Tortoise, Cinderella). One traditional role of the journalist is to defend the rights of the little person-the soldier against the unjust officer, the innocent man against false charges, the poor against exploitation.

Religion: There are two types of religious news story. First, there are events involving people's religious lives, such as the building of a new church or a pilgrimage. Second, there are statements by religious leaders on moral and spiritual affairs, such as contraception or salvation. It is important for the journalist to be aware of the relative numerical strengths of Christianity, Islam and other religions-including traditional local beliefs-in his or her country. The importance of a statement by a religious leader in your society depends both upon the news value of what he has to say and upon the size of his following.

Famous people: Prominent men and women make news. What people in the public eye do, the lives they lead and what they look like, are all of interest. It is especially newsworthy when they fall from power, lose their money or are involved in scandal.

Health: Many people are concerned with their health, so they are interested in stories about traditional remedies, medical research, diseases, hospitals and clinics, drugs, diet and exercise.

Sex: All societies are interested in sex, even if they do not talk about it openly. Many news stories about sex involve behaviour which goes outside society's generally accepted standards.

Weather: The weather may affect the daily routine of people and is of interest when it behaves unusually, with exceptionally high or low temperatures, or exceptionally high or low rainfall.

Food and drink: The rich person plans feasts, the poor person wants enough to eat and drink. Shortages and gluts, crop diseases and harvest sizes, prices of food in the market or the launch of a new brand of beer-these all make news.

Entertainment: Stories about music, dance, theatre, cinema and carving keep us informed of developments in the arts, who is doing what, who is performing where, and what it is worth going to see or hear.

Sport: Many people participate in sport and many others are spectators. They all want to know sports results, news of sportsmen and sportswomen and their achievements.

Human interest: There are often unusual and interesting aspects of other people's lives which are not particularly significant to society as a whole. Stories about these are called human interest stories.

Examples might be a child going abroad for surgery; a pilot recovering from injuries received in an air crash and determined to fly again; or a man with a collection of a million picture postcards.

News and Entertainment

Most people agree that the purpose of the news media-newspapers, magazines, radio and television-is to inform, to educate and to entertain. However, the purpose of the news itself is to inform and to educate your readers, listeners or viewers.

The entertainment can come from other areas-music and drama programs on radio; cartoons and crossword puzzles in newspapers. It is not the job of news to entertain.

This does not mean that news should be dull. If a news event has an element of humour, you should always try to write the story in a way to amuse your readers or listeners.

Nevertheless, the news should only be reported if it is real news. Do not report non-news as if it was news only because the story is entertaining.

As you gain more experience, you may be able to write things which are purely entertaining-such as a humorous look at current events. This is not news, however, and should not be presented as if it was. Make it clear to your readers or listeners what is news and what is not.

To Summarise: To decide what you should report, you must sort out news from non-news. To do this, ask yourself the following questions about anything you think may be news:

- *Is it new?*
- *Is it unusual?*
- *Is it interesting?*
- *Is it significant?*
- *Is it about people?*

To decide how to report it, ask yourself the following question:

- *How does this affect my readers', listeners' or viewers' lives?*

If it is not new or unusual, if it is not interesting or significant, and if it will not affect your readers' or listeners' lives, then it is not news. Do not publish it or broadcast it as news.

Scriptwriting

Guidelines

Can a contractor build an office building without being able to understand the architect's blueprints? Not likely. In the same way, key production personnel must understand the basics of scripts before they can create a production.

A comprehensive guide to scriptwriting is beyond the scope of this course. However, when you complete this module, you should understand the basic elements of scripts and even have a good start on writing one. (Remember: the most travelled route to producing is through writing.) Although you can learn the basics of writing here or in a good book, you can become a good writer only by writing.

Doing Lots of Writing

Most successful writers spend years writing before they start "getting it right" — at least right enough to start making money consistently.

In a sense, initial failures aren't failures at all; they're a prerequisite for success.

Thomas Edison said, "Genius is one percent inspiration and ninety-nine percent perspiration."

By another definition, *a genius* is a talented person who has done all his or her homework. These modules constitute the prerequisite homework involved in success. Keep in mind that writing for the electronic media is not the same as writing for print. Those who write for print enjoy some advantages their broadcast counterparts don't have. For example, a reader can go back and reread a sentence. If a sentence isn't understood in a TV production, however, the meaning is lost — or worse, the listener is distracted while figuring out what was said.

In order to deliver narration in a conversational style, you don't always follow standard rules of punctuation. Ellipses...three dots...are commonly used to designate pauses. Often, complete sentences aren't used...just as they aren't used in normal conversation. In broadcast writing an extra helping of commas provides clues to phrasing.

Although such usage is sometimes inconsistent with proper written form and your English 101 teacher may not approve, the overriding consideration in writing narration is *clarity*. This entails making it easy for an announcer to read, and making it easy for an audience to understand.

The way we perceive verbal information also complicates things.

When we read, we see words in groups or thought patterns. This helps us grasp the meaning.

But, when we listen, information is delivered one word at a time.

To make sense out of a sentence we must retain the first words in memory while adding all subsequent words to them, until the sentence or thought is complete.

If the sentence is too complex or takes too long to unfold, meaning is missed or confused.

Of course, through proper phrasing and word emphasis a narrator can go a long way toward ensuring understanding. This gives the spoken word a major advantage over the written word.

Broadcast Style

Writers write video scripts in broadcast style. With allowance for sentence variety, video scripts use short, concise, direct sentences — weeding out unnecessary words.

You should also be aware of [2]%some common mistakes, such as the difference between *further* and *farther* and *less than* and *fewer than.*

Of course, the English language is constantly changing. Things which were deemed "wrong" at one point can eventually come into regular use and become accepted.

"Close proximity" is becoming accepted, even though *proximity* means *close,* so it's actually redundant.

"There are less concerns about good grammar in advertising" should be "fewer concerns." *Fewer* relates to things you can count; *less* to things you can't. "Whom," even when correctly used in speech, now sounds stilted. "Irregardless" can be found in a couple of dictionaries — even though it's not seen as *acceptable.*

In writing your scripts, remember that the active voice is preferred over the inactive or passive voice. Nouns and verbs are preferred over adjectives, and specific words over general ones.

Facts must be taut, verbs strong and active; a script should crackle.

Avoid dependent clauses at the beginning of sentences. Attribution should come at the beginning of sentences ("According to the Surgeon General...") rather than at the end, which is common in newspaper writing. In broadcast style, we want to know from the beginning who's doing the "saying."

Ten Newswriting Guidelines

1. While making sure you bring the most interesting and surprising elements to the forefront of your story, don't give away everything right at the beginning. Maintain interest by spreading these "nuggets" throughout the story. And try not to let the lead-in to the story steal the thunder from what follows.
2. Use the active voice: subject, verb, and object.
3. Remember that nouns and verbs are stronger than adjectives and adverbs. Don't tell viewers what they

should be feeling by using adjectives, especially shopworn adjectives, such as "tragic," "amazing," and "stunning." If the story's facts don't make such things obvious, you might want to examine your approach.

4. Avoid jargon; use well-known terms. For example, your audience probably won't know what *ENG* and *B-roll* mean.
5. Include defining details, such as the make of the car and the type of trees being cut down.
6. Write (tell!) the story as if you were trying to catch the interest of a friend. Try mentally to follow up on the phrases, "Guess what...," or "This may be hard to believe, but...."
7. After you write something, set it aside for at least ten minutes and concentrate on something else. Then go back and review the story with a fresh perspective.
8. Read the story aloud (not under your breath).

Rewrite:

- sentences that are too long
- tongue-twisting or awkward phrases
- phrases that could be taken two ways
- long titles ("The 18-year-old, College Park Central High School sophomore...")

9. Don't rely on the sound track to tell the story or explain the video. The basic idea should be obvious from the video. At the same time, the audio and video should complement and strengthen each other.
10. Screen the complete audio and video story (package) as a "doubting Thomas." Have you made statements that could legitimately be challenged? Your clearly stated and verified facts should silence any rational critic.

Correlate Audio and Video

Keep in mind the basic guideline of correlating (relating) audio and video because viewers are accustomed to having what they *see* on the screen relate to what they *hear* — generally in the form of dialogue or narration. (Note that the intentionally long and complex sentence you just read is not be appropriate for broadcast style.) Even though you want audio and video to relate, watch out for the "see Dick run" approach where the audio states the obvious. If you can clearly see what's happening on the screen, this can get downright annoying.

Although radio drama had to slip many things into the dialogue to tip off the listeners to what they couldn't see ("Emma, why are you staring out the window?"), this is hardly the case with TV, where you can see what's taking place.

The trick is to write slightly off the pictures. This means that, while you don't describe the pictures, your words aren't so far removed from what is being seen that you split viewer attention. This technique involves a delicate balancing act.

Information Overload

With more than one hundred TV channels available to viewers in some areas and millions of pages of information available on the Internet, to name just two sources of information, one of today's biggest problems is information overload.

In TV production the goal is not just to unload information on viewers. To be successful you must engage your audience and clearly communicate selected information in a manner that will both enlighten and possibly even entertain.

We can absorb only a limited amount of information at a time. The average viewer has preconceptions and internal and external distractions that get in the way.

If a script is packed with too many facts, or if the information is not clearly presented, the viewer will become confused, lost, and frustrated.

Lost vs. Bored

Not only is the *amount* of information you communicate important, but also the *rate* at which it's presented. In information-centred productions, give the viewer a chance to process each idea before moving on to the next. If you move too rapidly, you'll lose your audience; too slowly, and you'll bore them.

The best approach in presenting crucial information in an instructional production is first to signal the viewer that something important is coming.

Next, present the information as simply and clearly as possible.

Then, reinforce may points by repeating them in a different way — or with an illustration or two.

Here are seven general rules to remember in writing for television. Some of these apply to instructional productions, some to dramatic productions, and some to both.

- Assume a conversational tone by using short sentences and an informal, approachable style.
- Engage your audience emotionally; make them care about both the people and content of your production.
- Provide adequate logical structure; let viewers know where you're going, which concepts are key, and when you're going to change the subject.
- After making an important point, expound on it; illustrate it.
- Don't try to pack too many facts into one program.
- Give your audience a chance to digest one concept before jumping to another.
- Pace your presentation according to the ability of your target audience to grasp the concepts.

Video Grammar

Some people say that, unlike writing, video and film production don't have standardized grammar (e.g., conventions or structure).

Although video has abandoned much of the grammar established by early filmmaking, even in this MTV, YouTube era we can use various techniques to add structure to formal productions.

In dramatic productions, lap-dissolves (when two video sources overlap for a few seconds during the transition from one to the other) often signal a change in time or place.

Fade-ins and fade-outs, which apply to both audio and video, can be likened to the beginning and end of book chapters. A fade-out consists of a two-or three-second transition from a full signal to black and silence. A fade-in is the reverse.

Fade-ins and fade-outs often signal a major change or division in a production, such as a major passage of time. (But "often" is a long way from "always.")

Traditionally, teleplays (television plays) and screenplays (film scripts) start with a fade-in and close with a fade-out.

Although we don't focus on dramatic film scripts here, one film writer-producer told us about a saying he has taped over his desk: *'It's the story, stupid.'*

Script Terms and Abbreviations

A number of terms and abbreviations are used in scriptwriting. Some describe camera movements.

When the entire camera is moved toward or away from the subject, it's referred to as a dolly.

A zoom, an optical version of a dolly, achieves somewhat the same effect. A script notation might say, "Camera zooms in for close-up of John" or "Camera zooms out to show John is not alone." A lateral move is a truck. Note the illustration on the left. Some terms designate shots.

Cuts or takes are instant transitions from one video source to another. In grammatical terms, shots can be likened to sentences where each shot is a visual statement.

The cover shot or establishing shot are designated on a script by "wide-shot" (WS) or "long shot" (LS). Occasionally, the abbreviations XLS for extreme long shot or VLS for very long shot are used. These all can give the audience a basic orientation to the geography of a scene (i.e., who is standing where) after which you'll cut to closer shots.

In the relatively low-resolution medium of standard-definition television (SDTV), this type of shot is visually weak because important details aren't easy to see. Film and HDTV (high-definition television) don't have quite the same problem.

Cover or establishing shots should be held only long enough to orient viewers to the relationship between major scene elements. Thereafter, they can be momentarily used as reminders or updates on scene changes as *reestablishing shots*.

Never Cling to the Familiar & Complain when Styles Change

Television needs more good writers. Somebody's gotta tell the little people that live in that box what to say and when to say it, and that, my friends, is where you come in!

There's not a person writing television today who didn't start off sitting alone at their desk, wondering who the heck they were trying to fool. What makes them special is that they started. They slogged through it. And they finished. Turns out, the best-kept secret in television is *keep writing*. Remember that, and you'll be sipping lattes with Tina Fey before you can say "rural juror." (It's a toughie.)

If you've never written a TV script before, fear not—as you move through the pointers below, you'll probably realize that most of them are already second nature. Like the Beatles song catalog or the spectrum of colors in a bag of M&Ms, there's a good chance TV writing structure is already ingrained in the recesses of your psyche. All those Saturday nights spent indoors on the couch in front of the boob tube are no longer hours wasted. Oh, no. You were doing *research*, and all that hard work is about to pay off!

Steps to Serious TV Writing Mastery

Watch more TV: Before getting started, you might want to grab yourself a notebook and couple of pens. Then slip into something comfy, roll onto the couch, and get to work. Watch everything. Watch anything. This is your opportunity to catch up on that TIVO list, or upgrade to the five-a-month Netflix plan. Try to see as many episodes of your favourite shows as possible, and even sludge through a few that you hate. But don't let yourself drift into that magical, mushy, sunken-eye dysphoria that we've all experienced after a couple of hours in front of the tube. If you're seeing stars, or having trouble remembering your children's names, then it's time to turn it off. Remember—this is your *homework*, and your job number-one is to *stay engaged*.

As you watch, write down interesting plot points or dialogue that seems especially funny or effective. Ask yourself questions, such as: Why did I laugh at that joke? Why did I break a sweat just before that commercial break? Why did I get bored and flip the channel? Write down your thoughts. This will be an essential reference as you delve into your own material and work to create scenarios that will affect your audience in the same ways that you were affected. By logging your responses, you'll also gain insight into your own likes and dislikes, and this will be an especially useful tool in choosing your script genre and format. So get to it! Grab that popcorn, flip open your notebook, and get ready to indulge in hours-upon-hours of guilt-free TV!

To Spec or not to Spec: Ten years ago, if you wanted to be a TV scribe, there was just one way to break into the 'biz. You had to start by writing two or more fake episodes for existing shows on 'speculation' of purchase, or 'on spec.' Then you would try to get these scripts into the hands of the show's head writers, and hope they liked them enough to hire you on as a freelancer (or, in special cases, as a staff writer for the show). After years of proving yourself, you might break out on your own by penning a 'pilot' script for an original series, and if this got picked up, you stood a chance of becoming a 'showrunner' of your own show.

That was then. This is now. Today, literary agents and development execs are just as likely to ask an unproven writer for a pilot script as they are for a spec. Some development folk even prefer pilots to spec scripts, as pilot scripts tend to show off the unique voice of a new writer, rather than his or her ability to copy someone else's.

The spec still has its place, however, and many new writers still use them as a way to compare their writing to that of professionals, or to show off their talents in varying genres. Writing a spec can also be easier than scripting an original show, since you don't need to set up the characters or their world. If you were to write a spec for *Buffy the Vampire Slayer*, for instance, you could start right out with Buffy and Angel swapping spit and lounging in a tomb without explaining that a) Angel is a vampire with a soul, b) Buffy is a slayer in love with a vampire, and c) tombs are perfectly desirable locales for these types of romances. In a spec, you can assume your readers already know the show, and can jump right in and get to the good stuff! So, the first decision you must make is whether to write a spec or an original pilot. Each will be a useful tool in marketing yourself as a writer, so the question really comes down to you. Have you thought up the perfect offbeat scenario for *Kath & Kim*, or do you want to pitch the next great cop show to fill the vacuum left by *The Wire*? Hey—with a 100 pages to write, why not do both?

Know Your Show: If you're thinking about writing a spec, start by focusing on the on the newest, freshest, mostly highly-rated shows within a genre that you love. A sitcom today is not a sitcom in 1990. No one wants to read a brand-spanking-new episode of *Alf*. Your spec must be of a current television show *still in production*, and hopefully one that will be on air three years from now, so that your script will continue to feel current. A program like *The Simpsons* is a popular spec because that show will be in production well after Chelsea Clinton has launched her presidential bid. And that's what you want—a show with legs, that is tightly written and well-known to would-be readers. Some popular choices right now are *30 Rock, Pushing Daisies,* and *Mad Men*.

Once you've targeted a show, try to get your hands on a written episode. Google will serve you well here, as will websites like dailyscript.com and hollywoodbookcity.com. If you have a cousin working nights at CBS, now would also be the time to give her a call! Do whatever you can to track down an episode of your show. The formatting idiosyncrasies of your show should be reproduced in your spec, and you're gonna need a script to know what those are. Unlike movie scripts, all TV shows are formatted differently, and you want your spec to *look* like a real episode as much as you want it to *read* like one. Templates for many current shows are also packaged with screenwriting software such as Final Draft and Screenwriter, but you'll still want to see a real script to get a sense of how it reads on the page.

If, on the other hand, you plan to write your very own pilot, start by watching every show within your genre currently making waves. Make note of how they're structured, when the commercial breaks arrive in a half-hour versus one-hour show, and what types of themes and situations comprise the main storylines. Television is a lot like the fashion industry, and the writing styles and storylines of new shows may vary radically from the season before. When pitching TV, you never want to show up on the runway wearing MC Hammer pants and a hip pouch. Try to get a handle on your subject, and know how your pilot is *similar* and *different* from current shows in its genre.

Know Your Audience: One huge difference between writing movies and writing for TV is that when writing for the small screen, you need to constantly consider the attention span of your audience. Think about it—a movie audience has bought their $10 ticket and is essentially locked into their seats for the next two hours. They can't switch channels. They can't wander off into kitchen, or answer the phone. Not so in TV! As a matter of fact, many people seem to be looking for a reason *to* switch the channel. There are just so many other choices—surely there must be something on more entertaining than *this.*

To make sure you're keeping your audience's attention you need to first know who your audience *is*. And how do you do that? Watch the commercials! Marketing firms are spending millions of dollars as we speak, making sure the right ads are matched to shows delivering products to the right consumers. If you're writing a spec, what types of actors appear in the commercials? Who are they targeting? If you're writing a pilot, watch the commercials of your would-be competitors. Are they Doritos ads, or investment banking commercials? Are they selling detergent or Legos? You can learn a lot about a show by knowing who's watching it.

Get on Pitch: Alright—you've chosen your spec show, or figured out your angle for the next great sitcom. You've alienated family and neighbours staying up all night catching reruns, and now you're ready for the fun part—writing!

Hmmm. Maybe just one more cup of Red Zinger, and THEN the writing... If you're having trouble getting going, you may need to take a big step back, and ask yourself what your episode is really about. In fact, if you can't summarize your entire script in just one or two sentences, then you're probably not ready to start writing. In Hollywoodland, they call this the 'pitch', and it's what creative execs will ask you for in the fifteen-second elevator ride after you've introduced yourself as a TV writer. "What's the *pitch*," the kind ones will say—and you better get it all out before that bell rings for the lobby!

A good pitch should tell the entire plot of your pilot or spec, including essential character traits or flaws, in less time that it takes to eat a mini scone at Starbucks. It should have a clear beginning, middle, and end, and will usually start by introducing the main character:

- An absentee father whose life is plagued by mistakes...
- Then describing the character's journey:
- *Finds himself sent back in time at random intervals...*
- And finishes by summarizing with an unexpected outcome:

Only to discover he's been sent on a mission to protect the world, and along the way will be given the opportunity to correct the ills of his past.

This is not just an exercise in preparedness—sharpening your pitch will force you to boil your episode down to its core elements, and you'll ultimately end up with a better script. Some writers even start with a great pitch, then work backwards to flesh it out into a show. Whatever your approach, make sure to get on pitch early in the process—it'll make your own journey much more enjoyable.

What A Character! Television is a lot of things, but one thing it definitely ain't is subtle. In movies, major plot points may happen off-screen, and key characters may spend good chunks of the movie mulling over big decisions in relative silence. Not so in TV! In fact, one of the major differences between the mediums is the in-your-facedness of television—almost nothing is left open for interpretation, and major plot points always play out on-screen, in full view of their hungry audiences. Always remember your viewer's remote control, sitting there on his coffee table, beckoning.

One of the ways television writers keep their audience's hooked is through the creation of *very strong characters*. When deciding upon your cast for a new pilot, try to make each character as radically *different* from one another as you possibly can. A great example of this is the NBC show *30 Rock*. Think about the characters that comprise Tina Fey's group of trusted (and politically incorrect) scribes: A slobby man-child, a cocky overeducated African-American, a dorky impressionist, an effete soccer dad, and Tina Fey herself—a 42-year-old workaholic with no social life and an addiction to fast food. Just in naming the archetypes, you can see the potential for conflict and humor when these dueling personas are stuck together in a writing room. Add in a Donald Trump-styled boss, a straight-off-the bus office page, and the dueling personalities of a couple of hot-headed actors, and you have yourself one heck of a funny half-hour!

So how do you draft a taster's choice of well-defined characters that'll carry your show through several seasons of shifting plotlines and gripping drama? Two tricks in particular are well-used by seasoned writers. First—*write who you know, but without the boring stuff*. Drop your dad, or your girlfriend, or your sixth-grade math teach into the mix, and see how they fare next to your shape-shifting alien or talking dog. Second—*take characters from other TV shows and interject them into your own.* If you're looking for the perfect working-dad, why not Peter from *Family Guy*? Or Charlie from *Two and a Half Men*? Borrowing characters can be a great way to define the dynamics of your cast and to sharpen your overall vision. And don't worry—as your script develops, these kidnapees will take on their own personalities and become your own. So have fun! Pick and choose as you please—these tricks will make developing characters easier, and should expose the strengths and weaknesses in your supporting cast.

For those of you writing the next great episode of *Ashes to Ashes*, writing a spec demands it's own homework. Sure—a good amount of the upfront work has been done for you, as any show worth specking should already have a well-defined menagerie of misfits.

Your job now is to get to know them better the writers who birthed 'em. Try writing a page from the point-of-view of each character that discusses their lives and their conflicts with other people on the show. Knowing your characters inside and out is foundational to good story structure and dialogue. So do the work! It will be invaluable as you charge headlong into your script.

Whether you're piloting or specking, one final thing to keep in mind about great television characters is that they *never change*. If you've watched an HBO season finale recently you may have spotted the rare exception, but this rule holds true 99.5% of the time.

This isn't a movie—your characters can *learn*, but they should not be allowed to *grow* in any significant way. What they figure out in one episode should usually be forgot by the next. TV characters should be crystal clear and set up in obvious conflict with others from the pilot onwards. A TV writer's job is to maintain this initial dynamic, sometimes against all odds. If you're writing a spec, do not try to take the show in a bold new direction—stick to the characters the way they are, and find a brand-new scenario in which their personalities and attitudes will still be intact at curtains down.

House Of Cards: If you've pulled together a rough outline of your show and mapped out each of your central characters, you may be thinking "now what?" How do I make all these cool characters and super-sweet plot points fit within a half-hour script? Structuring a script can seem like a house of cards, but don't let it! Take a deep breath, pull out that notebook, and keep reading. In short order this will all seem about as easy as finding the treat in a box of Cracker Jacks.

Whatever type of script you're writing, it's helpful to think about your story in terms of a numbers of *acts* stuck between a series of commercial breaks. Most programs also begin with a short, highly-comedic or highly-dramatic *teaser* which stands alone from the rest of the episode, but also sets up the main storyline or theme of the script. Many shows also end with a similarly short outtro that pays off a lingering joke or plot point, called a *tag*.

Half-hour sitcoms tend to unfold in the following manner:

Teaser—commercial—Act I—commercial—Act II—commercial—tag.

Whereas hour-long shows usually unfold like so:

Teaser—com—Act I—com—Act II—com—Act III—com—Act IV—com—tag.

The first act in a TV show tends to be longer than the final acts, and in half-hour programs there are usually 15-18 scenes in the overall show. In hour-long programs that number raises to around 25. The teaser and the tag are usually comprised of just 1-3 scenes each.

The rule of thumb is that one page of writing generally equals just under one minute of air time, so hour-long dramas tend to be about 60-70 pages long, and half-hour network shows tend to be about 40-50 pages. If that math seems crazy, check the section HOW TO FORMAT A TV SCRIPT to learn about the strange spacing rules of certain kinds of scripts.

Shows that are written for cable (and don't need to be timed out with commercial breaks) tend to be longer, but the act-break structure is usually handled in exactly the same way, in part because many cable shows will end up in syndication on other stations.

Learn Your A, B, Cs: Before you figure out what story points should fit within each of your acts, it'll be helpful to think about your script as travelling down two or three separate roads at the same time.

You're first road is called your *A-plot*, and it is that part of your script which fuels the actions of the main characters in the script, and generally pushes the story along, as in: *Oh no, the city is under attack—thank goodness the Power Rangers are here to fight the monster and save us all!* Your *B-plot* is that part of your script which expresses the emotional entanglements and problems of your main characters tangentially to the doomsday scenario that is unfolding, as in: *Carrie Bradshaw's life may be in ruins, but wait—who in the world is that dreamboat? Let me date him and report back to my friends!* Hour-long shows will usually also have a *C-plot*, which focuses on the parallel lives of supporting characters, as in: *Tony Soprano's daughter Meadow rebels against her family by dating a Jewish African-American student at Columbia!*

Each of your acts should contain a 60/30/10 breakdown of your A, B and C-plots, respectively. In a half hour show with no C-plot, the ratio should be closer to 60/40. These are rough estimates, however, and you should feel free to take liberties in how you organize your story. The bottom line is to *keep your show moving.*

If the A, B, Cs are negotiable, this next rule is not: Each act *must* end in a genuine 'cliffhanger.' Act breaks are the scariest part of writing, 'cause this is where you're gonna lose your audience if they're not constructed carefully. A cliffhanger can be an 'A-plot cliffhanger,' such as when a main character has just been shot or gotten themselves fired for showing up to work naked, or it can be a 'B-plot cliffhanger,' such as when your protagonist has just been kissed by her long-term crush, or her estranged mother has shown up unannounced. Whether your cliffhangers are *plot-based* or *emotional*, they always need to be there, right smack dab at the end of every act. Always arrange your scenes so that your big, juicy, flashing-question-mark-moments fall just before your breaks.

Talk The Talk: Before worrying about how to make your characters talk like they're in a TV show, you'll need to give them something to talk *about*. Honestly—this is the best advice on dialogue writing you'll ever hear.

Don't ever find yourself in a situation where you're trying to come up with clever lines without first being sure of what each of your characters really *want*. If you know your characters inside and out and know what their individual goals are in every scene, your dialogue will begin to write itself. Seriously—you can just sit on your hands and watch it roll out on the screen!

Okay, maybe not. But if you remind yourself what each of your characters are *trying to get* before heading into every scene, you'll find writing dialogue is a whole lot easier than it seems. That doesn't mean they should come right out and say it! Oh—they should lie, and tease, flirt and manipulate just like the rest of us. But know what they *really* want underneath it all—even if it's never gonna happen.

Now sprinkle in some conflict, and you're done! The smartest drama and the wittiest comedy always come from situations of high conflict, and you need to make sure you've got a healthy dose of this in every single scene.

The best way to bring your conflict to a boiling point is to set up each of your characters' *wants* in direct conflict to every other character. Now they have a reason to talk to one another, and with their conflicting motivations, they'll push and pull at each other as both try to have it their own way. Add in a couple jokes and a few smart-alecky references, and you've got television!

Almost. Like all aspects of TV writing, there is very little room for subtlety, and your dialogue should never feel, well... *boring*. There is a real difference between "dialogue" and "conversation," and especially when writing television, your characters should be just a little sharper, brighter, and quicker than most of us are in real life.

Lastly, always be sure to *read your lines out loud*. You're not writing a novel—these words are meant to be performed by actors, and you may be surprised by how differently dialogue can play outside of your head. If you're brave, invite a friend to read your script for you, and simply *listen* to how your script plays out when spoken. You may love it, or you may want to throw your laptop out the window and move to another country. Either way, you'll end up with a stronger script!

Big Picture: These days, most television shows are *serialized*, meaning they have season arcs in which several storylines carry through from one episode to the next. If you had been a staff writer on *Extras*, you might have been up all night worrying about how Andy's transformation from extra to sitcom-star might affect the unique brand of outcast-humor that made the first season of this show so successful.

That is not your job as a spec-writer! Your original spec should seem loosely referential to the most-recent season of your show, but don't get bogged down in the specifics. If Brent LeRoy has decided to become a vegetarian on a recent episode of *Corner Gas*, he can certainly relish a plate of eggs and sausage in your script!

Pilots are a different story. Your original half-hour show featuring a gang of multi-ethnic teens poised to take over the world of professional eating must be *cohesive* and *foundational* at the same time.

Your script should have a clear beginning, middle, and end, but also introduce a paradigm that will seem compelling for seasons to come. That is the real trick in pilot writing—how to create a script that introduces all of your characters within a concise episode, but also exposes a can of worms that will demand resolution in show after show after show. Sarah and John may have blown-up the terminator in the pilot for *The Sarah Connor Chronicles*, but it's the enduring existence of Skynet that motivates the rest of the season!

The Fun Is In The: If you can't finish this sentence, then stop writing, grab your bathing suit, run to the beach (or bathtub) and do your best somersault into an oncoming wave! Writing should be fun! Sure, there's the low times, the dull times, the frustrating times, and the times you want to use your script as kindling—but somewhere deep inside of you, remember why you bit this donkey in the first place. Because you get to make up a whole world of characters, problems, and good times. Because you're funny, and you want the world to know it.

Because your job sucks, and being a TV writer is way more exciting than handling HR for a mortgage bank. Whatever your reasons for starting down this path, they probably haven't changed. Writing is awesome. And you're awesome for wanting to be a writer. So no more procrastination! Back at it, my friend! You're almost there—just ninety-nine and a half pages left to go...

5

The Basic of News Broadcasting in India

The Constitution of India guarantees to all its citizens, the right to free speech, which right has been liberally construed by our Supreme Court as encompassing not just the freedom of press, but also the right of the citizen to be informed of matters of public moment and concern. The fundamental premise of a democracy is the accountability of all its institutions to the political sovereign, viz the people.

It is axiomatic that for democracy to survive and flourish, freedom must live in the hearts of people, and the citizenry must be ever vigilant against all attempts to subvert the rule of law. Democracies have decayed into anarchy not merely on account of major events such as coups, but also by insidious erosion caused by egregious corruption and abuse of power. Exposing the threat within itself has become one of the most important roles of the news media, particularly the electronic media whose reach and penetration has the promise to make democracy a living reality for those who do not have access to the print media for want of literacy or otherwise, and giving them a sense of involvement in the process of governance. India is the world's largest democracy, demographically marked by diversity in religion, language and caste, and undoubtedly has problems that are significantly peculiar to it. Yet at the same time, it shares certain common values with other vibrant democracies, and one of them is balancing the freedom of the press with putting in place checks and balances that seek to instill a sense of responsibility and to prevent abuse of this freedom, without the "chilling effect" that would impair journalistic freedom.

It is the duty of media to keep the citizenry informed of the state of governance, which mostly puts it at odds with the establishment. A media that is meant to expose the lapses in government and in public life cannot obviously be regulated by government – it would lack credibility. It is a fundamental paradigm of freedom of speech that media must be free from governmental control in the matter of "content" – censorship and free speech are sworn enemies. It therefore falls upon the journalist profession to evolve institutional checks and safeguards, specific to the electronic media that can define the path that would conform to the highest standards of rectitude and journalistic ethics and guide the media in the discharge of its solemn constitutional duty.

There are models of self governance evolved in other countries who have seen an evolution of the electronic media including the news media much before it developed in India. The remarkable feature of all these models is self governance, and a monitoring by a "jury of its peers". There are undoubtedly limitations in any model of self governance in which compliance is entirely voluntary.

However this does not suggest that such models are ineffective. Their efficacy flows from the fact that the basic strength of a news channel lies in its credibility, from which flows its ability to influence public opinion. A censure emanating from a jury of its peers would indisputably affect the credibility of a channel. Besides, such a process is not without its legal ramifications. One of the important defenses to civil and criminal actions (based on defamation) is "fair comment" and bona fide attempts to unravel the truth.

The difference between inaccuracy and falsehood lies many a time in the motive. Channel acting in breach of established guidelines could hardly defend its motives or suggest that it was acting fairly, if it is censured by a jury of its peers. The interference by the government, however well intentioned, would imperil not just this method of independent journalism, but the very process of investigation itself. It therefore has become imperative that the news channels lay down guidelines, procedural safeguards and establish a body that would act as a watchdog and a grievance redressal forum.

Section-1 : Fundamental Principles

Professional electronic journalists should accept and understand that they operate as trustees of public and should, therefore, make it their mission to seek the truth and to report it fairly with integrity and independence. Professional journalists should stand fully accountable for their actions. The purpose of this code is to document the broad paradigms accepted by the members of the News Broadcasters Association (NBA) as practice and procedures that would help journalists of electronic media to adhere to the highest possible standards of public service and integrity.

News channels recognize that they have a special responsibility in the matter of adhering to high standards of journalism since they have the most potent influence on public opinion. The broad principles on which the news channels should function are, therefore, as stated hereinafter.

Broadcasters shall, in particular, ensure that they do not select news for the purpose of either promoting or hindering either side of any controversial public issue. News shall not be selected or designed to promote any particular belief, opinion or desires of any interest group.

The fundamental purpose of dissemination of news in a democracy is to educate and inform the people of the happenings in the country, so that the people of the country understand significant events and form their own conclusions.

Broadcasters shall ensure a full and fair presentation of news as the same is the fundamental responsibility of each news channel. Realizing the importance of presenting all points of view in a democracy, the broadcasters should, therefore, take responsibility in ensuring that controversial subjects are fairly presented, with time being allotted fairly to each point of view. Besides, the selection of items of news shall also be governed by public interest and importance based on the significance of these items of news in a democracy.

Section-2 : Principles of Self Regulation

The News Broadcasters Association (NBA) has established commonly accepted content guidelines as a way of practicing self regulation. The purpose is to define editorial principles which are consistent with the tenets of the freedom of speech articulated in the constitution of India; the regulatory framework; common sensibilities of television viewers.

The purpose of these principles of self regulation is to serve as an affirmative declaration of understanding of, and compliance with, the basic values and objectives that news channels enshrine.

It is to ensure that these principles are observed in spirit, and not just in the letter.

The purpose of putting together the principles of self regulation is to avoid compromising the genre of television news by broadcasting content that is malicious, biased, regressive, knowingly inaccurate, hurtful, misleading, or aimed at willfully concealing a conflict of interest.

The purpose of these principles of self regulation is to empower the profession of television journalism by an abiding set of values, which will stand the test of time, and ensure that balanced and comprehensive journalism flourishes, to strengthen India's democracy Detailed below are some of the areas where the broadcasters seek to self-regulate.

Accuracy is at the heart of the news television business. Viewers of 24 hour news channels expect speed, but it is the responsibility of TV news channels to keep accuracy, and balance, as precedence over speed. If despite this there are errors, channels should be transparent about them. Errors must be corrected promptly and clearly, whether in the use of pictures, a news report, a caption, a graphic or a script. Channels should also strive not to broadcast anything which is obviously defamatory or libelous. Truth will be a defence in all cases where a larger public interest is involved, and in even these cases, equal opportunities will be provided for individuals involved to present their point of view. This also applies in cases where television channels report on those holding public office, though by virtue of doing so, no person can claim immunity from scrutiny from or criticism by news channels.

Ensuring neutrality: TV News channels must provide for neutrality by offering equality for all affected parties, players and actors in any dispute or conflict to present their point of view. Though neutrality does not always come down to giving equal space to all sides (news channels shall strive to give main view points of the main parties)news channels must strive to ensure that allegations are not portrayed as fact and charges are not conveyed as an act of guilt.

Reporting on crime and safeguards to ensure crime and violence are not glorified: Television news has greater reach, and more immediate impact than other forms of media, and this makes it all the more necessary that channels exercise restraint to ensure that any report or visuals broadcast do not induce, glorify, incite, or positively depict violence and its perpetrators, regardless of ideology or context. Specific care must be taken not to broadcast visuals that can be prejudicial or inflammatory. Equally, in the reporting of violence (whether collective or individual) the act of violence must not be glamorized, because it may have a misleading or desensitizing impact on viewers.

News channels will ensure that such reconstructions will not cross boundaries of good taste and sensibility. This includes taking adequate precaution while showing any visual instance of pain, fear or suffering, and visuals or details of methods of suicide and self harm of any kind and will not cross boundaries of good taste and decency.

Depiction of violence or intimidation against women and children: As an elaboration of Point 3, news channels will ensure that no woman or juvenile, who is a victim of sexual violence, aggression, trauma, or has been a witness to the same is shown on television without due effort taken to conceal the identity. In reporting all cases of sexual assault, or instances where the personal character or privacy of women are concerned, their names, pictures and other details will not be broadcast/ divulged. Similarly, the identity of victims of child abuse and juvenile delinquents will not be revealed, and their pictures will be morphed to conceal their identity.

Sex and nudity: News channels will ensure that they do not show, without morphing, nudity of the male or female form. Channels will also not show explicit images of sexual activity or sexual perversions or acts of sexual violence like rape or molestation, or show pornography, or the use of sexually suggestive language. (As a qualifier however, channels are not expected to be moralistic or prudish, and this self regulation is aimed not at moral policing, but rather at ensuring that overtly regressive and explicit acts and visuals do not slip into broadcasts).

Privacy: As a rule channels must not intrude on private lives, or personal affairs of individuals, unless there is a clearly established larger and identifiable public interest for such a broadcast. The underlying principle that news channels abide by is that the intrusion of the private spaces, records, transcripts, telephone conversations and any other material will not be for salacious interest, but only when warranted in the public interest. However, it is also understood that the pursuit of the truth and the news is not possible through the predetermined principle of prior permission; hence door stepping individuals or authorities for the purpose of newsgathering may be used only in the larger purpose of public interest.. Further, in the case of minors, in any broadcast that intrudes on their privacy, the channel should attempt, where possible, to seek the consent of the parent or legal guardian. However, the defence of the premise of privacy cannot be misconstrued as the denial of access, and this applies to all individuals, including those in the public eye and public personalities. It does however apply in its entirety, as per the provisions mentioned above, to their children and kin who are minors.

Endangering national security: In the use of any terminology or maps, that represent India and Indian strategic interests, all news channels will use specific terminology and maps mandated by law and Indian government rules. (The depiction of the map of the territory of India will reflect official guidelines, as detailed in official literature). News channels will also refrain from allowing broadcasts that encourage secessionist groups and interests, or reveal information that endangers lives and national security. However, it is in the public interest to broadcast instances of breach of national security and loopholes in national security and reporting these cannot be confused with endangering national security.

Refraining from advocating or encouraging superstition and occultism: News channels will not broadcast any material that glorifies superstition and occultism in any manner. In broadcasting any news about such genre, news channels will also issue public disclaimers to ensure that viewers are not misled into believing or emulating such beliefs and activity.

Therefore news channels will not broadcast "as fact" myths about "supernatural" acts, apparitions and ghosts, personal or social deviations or deviant behaviour, and recreations of the same. Wherever references are made to such cases, news channels will issue on air riders/disclaimers/warnings to ensure that such beliefs or events are not passed off "as fact" since they can hurt rational sensibilities.

Sting operations: As a guiding principle, sting and under cover operations should be a last resort of news channels in an attempt to give the viewer comprehensive coverage of any news story. News channels will not allow sex and sleaze as a means to carry out sting operations, the use of narcotics and psychotropic substances or any act of violence, intimidation, or discrimination as a justifiable means in the recording of any sting operation.

Sting operations, will also abide by the principles of self regulation mentioned above, and news channels will ensure that they will be guided, as mentioned above, by an identifiable larger public interest. News channels will as a ground rule, ensure that sting operations are carried out only as a tool for getting conclusive evidence of wrong doing or criminality, and that there is no deliberate alteration of visuals, or editing, or interposing done with the raw footage in a way that it also alters or misrepresents the truth or presents only a portion of the truth.

Corrigendum: All news channels will keeping with the principle of due accuracy and impartiality, ensure that significant mistakes made in the course of any broadcast is acknowledged and corrected on air immediately. Corrections should also be scheduled in such a way that they attract enough viewer attention and are not concealed. This, like the other principles, must be observed in spirit, and not just in letter, to avoid any compromise to the reputation of the news broadcasting industry in India.

Viewer feedback: All News Channels will on their website, create provision to receive consumer feedback. Further any specific viewer complaints will be responded to. In the event any news channel gets a specific complaint if found to be true it will admit to the same on air and will respond in fullness and fairness to the viewer. In the event, a viewer/body perceives prejudice by any specific report carried by the News channel, it will respond in fullness and without impartiality to the viewer.

The Broadcasting Industry

The Indian national television (Doordarshan) and radio (All India Radio, or Akashwani) networks are state-owned and managed by the Ministry of Information and Broadcasting. Their news reporting customarily presents the government's point of view. For example, coverage of the 1989 election campaign blatantly favoured the government of Rajiv Gandhi, and autonomy of the electronic media became a political issue. V.P. Singh's National Front government sponsored the Prasar Bharati (Indian Broadcasting) Act, which Parliament considered in 1990, to provide greater autonomy to Doordarshan and All India Radio. The changes that resulted were limited. The bill provided for the establishment of an autonomous corporation to run Doordarshan and All India Radio. The corporation was to operate under a board of governors to be in charge of appointments and policy and a broadcasting council to respond to complaints. However, the legislation required that the corporation prepare and submit its budget within the framework of the central budget and stipulated that the personnel of the new broadcasting corporation be career civil servants to facilitate continued government control. In the early 1990s, increasing competition from television broadcasts transmitted via satellite appeared the most effective manner of limiting the progovernment bias of the government-controlled electronic media.

Since the 1980s, India has experienced a rapid proliferation of television broadcasting that has helped shape popular culture and the course of politics. Although the first television program was broadcast in 1959, the expansion of television did not begin in earnest until the extremely popular telecast of the Ninth Asian Games, which were held in New Delhi in 1982.

Realizing the popular appeal and consequent influence of television broadcasting, the government undertook an expansion that by 1990 was planned to provide television access to 90 percent of the population. In 1993, about 169 million people were estimated to have watched Indian television each week, and, by 1994, it was reported that there were some 47 million households with televisions. There also is a growing selection of satellite transmission and cable services available.

Television programming was initially kept tightly under the control of the government, which embarked on a self-conscious effort to construct and propagate a cultural idea of the Indian nation.

This goal is especially clear in the broadcasts of such megaseries as the Hindu epics *Ramayana* and *Mahabharata*. In addition to the effort at nation-building, the politicians of India's ruling party have not hesitated to use television to build political support. In fact, the political abuse of Indian television led to demands to increase the autonomy of Doordarshan; these demands ultimately resulted in support for the Prasar Bharati Act.

The 1990s have brought a radical transformation of television in India. Transnational satellite broadcasting made its debut in January 1991, when owners of satellite dishes—initially mostly at major hotels—began receiving Cable News Network (CNN) coverage of the Persian Gulf War.

Three months later, Star TV began broadcasting via satellite. Its fare initially included serials such as "The Bold and the Beautiful" and MTV programs. Satellite broadcasting spread rapidly through India's cities as local entrepreneurs erected dishes to receive signals and transmitted them through local cable systems. After its October 1992 launch, Zee TV offered stiff competition to Star TV. However, the future of Star TV was bolstered by billionaire Rupert Murdock, who acquired the network for US$525 million in July 1993. CNN International, part of the Turner Broadcasting System, was slated to start broadcasting entertainment programs, including top Hollywood films, in 1995.

Competition from the satellite stations in India brought radical change to Doordarshan by cutting its audience and threatening its advertising revenues at a time when the government was pressuring it to pay for expenditures from internal revenues. In response, Doordarshan decided in 1993 to start five new channels in addition to its original National Channel. Programming was radically transformed, and controversial news shows, soap operas, and coverage of high-fashion events proliferated. Of the new Doordarshan channels, however, only the Metro Channel, which carries MTV music videos and other popular shows, has survived in the face of the new trend for talk programs that engage in a potpourri of racy topics.

Broadcast Communications in India

Indian Telecommunication industry, with about 525.65 million mobile phone connections (Oct. 2009), is the third largest telecommunication network in the world and the second largest in terms of number of wireless connections. For the past decade or so, telecommunication activities have gained momentum in India. Efforts have been made from both governmental and non-governmental platforms to enhance the infrastructure. The idea is to help modern telecommunication technologies to serve all segments of India's culturally diverse society, and to transform it into a country of technologically aware people.

Modern Growth

A large population, low telephony penetration levels, and a rise in consumers' income and spending owing to strong economic growth have helped make India the fastest-growing telecom market in the world. The first and largest operator is the state-owned incumbent BSNL, which is also the 7th largest telecom company in the world in terms of its number of subscribers. BSNL was created by corporatization of the erstwhile DTS (Department of Telecommunication Services), a government unit responsible for provision of telephony services. Subsequently, after the telecommunication policies were revised to allow private operators, companies such as Bharti Airtel, Tata Indicom, Vodafone, Idea Cellular, Aircel and Loop Mobile have entered the space, see major operators in India. In 2008-09, rural India outpaced urban India in mobile growth rate.

India's mobile phone market is the fastest growing in the world, with companies adding some 16.67 million new customers a month. The total number of telephones in the country crossed the 525 million mark on Oct. 2009. The overall tele-density has increased to 44.85% in Oct. 2009. In the wireless segment, 16.67 million subscribers have been added in Oct. 2009. The total wireless subscribers (GSM, CDMA & WLL (F)) base is more than 525.65 million now. The wireline segment subscriber base stood at 37.25 million with a decline of 0.05 million in Oct. 2009.

History

Telecom in the real sense means transfer of information between two distant points in space. The popular meaning of telecom always involves electrical signals and nowadays people exclude postal or any other raw telecommunication methods from its meaning. Therefore, the history of Indian telecom can be started with the introduction of telegraph.

Introduction of Telegraph

The postal and telecom sectors had a slow and uneasy start in India. In 1850, the first experimental electric telegraph Line was started between Kolkata and Diamond Harbour. In 1851, it was opened for the British East India Company. The Posts and Telegraphs department occupied a small corner of the Public Works Department, at that time.

Construction of 4,000 miles (6,400 km) of telegraph lines connecting Kolkata (Calcutta) and Peshawar in the north along with Agra, Mumbai (Bombay) through Sindwa Ghats, and Chennai in the south, as well as Ootacamund and Bangalore was started in November 1853. Dr. William O'Shaughnessy, who pioneered telegraph and telephone in India, belonged to the Public Works Department. He tried his level best for the development of telecom through out this period. A separate department was opened in 1854 when telegraph facilities were opened to the public.

Introduction of the Telephone

In 1880, two telephone companies namely The Oriental Telephone Company Ltd. and The Anglo-Indian Telephone Company Ltd. approached the Government of India to establish telephone exchanges in India. The permission was refused on the grounds that the establishment of telephones was a Government monopoly and that the Government itself would undertake the work.

By 1881, the Government changed its earlier decision and a licence was granted to the Oriental Telephone Company Limited of England for opening telephone exchanges at Kolkata, Mumbai, Chennai (Madras) and Ahmedabad. 28 January 1882, is a Red Letter Day in the history of telephone in India. On this day Major E. Baring, Member of the Governor General of India's Council declared open the Telephone Exchange in Kolkata, Chennai and Mumbai. The exchange at Kolkata named "Central Exchange" was opened at third floor of the building at 7, Council House Street. The Central Telephone Exchange had 93 number of subscribers. Bombay also witnessed the opening of Telephone Exchange in 1882.

Further Developments

- 1902-First wireless telegraph station established between Saugor Islands and Sandheads.
- 1907-First Central Battery of telephones introduced in Kanpur.
- 1913-1914-First Automatic Exchange installed in Shimla.
- 23 July 1927-Radio-telegraph system between the UK and India, with beam stations at Khadki and Daund, inaugurated by Lord Irwin by exchanging greetings with the King of England.
- 1933-Radiotelephone system inaugurated between the UK and India.
- 1953-12 channel carrier system introduced.
- 1960-First subscriber trunk dialing route commissioned between Kanpur and Lucknow.
- 1975-First PCM system commissioned between Mumbai City and Andheri telephone exchanges.
- 1976-First digital microwave junction introduced.
- 1979-First optical fibre system for local junction commissioned at Pune.
- 1980-First satellite earth station for domestic communications established at Secunderabad, A.P..
- 1983-First analog Stored Program Control exchange for trunk lines commissioned at Mumbai.
- 1984-C-DOT established for indigenous development and production of digital exchanges.
- 1985-First mobile telephone service started on non-commercial basis in Delhi.

While all the major cities and towns in the country were linked with telephones during the British period, the total number of telephones in 1948 was only around 80,000. Even after independence, growth was extremely slow. The telephone was a status symbol rather than being an instrument of utility.

The number of telephones grew leisurely to 980,000 in 1971, 2.15 million in 1981 and 5.07 million in 1991, the year economic reforms were initiated in the country.

While certain innovative steps were taken from time to time, as for example introduction of the telex service in Mumbai in 1953 and commissioning of the first [subscriber trunk dialing] route between Delhi and Kanpur in 1960, the first waves of change were set going by Sam Pitroda in the eighties. He brought in a whiff of fresh air. The real transformation in scenario came with the announcement of the National Telecom Policy in 1994.

Emergence as a Major Player

In 1975, the Department of Telecom (DoT) was separated from P&T. DoT was responsible for telecom services in entire country until 1985 when Mahanagar Telephone Nigam Limited (MTNL) was carved out of DoT to run the telecom services of Delhi and Mumbai. In 1990s the telecom sector was opened up by the Government for private investment as a part of Liberalisation-Privatization-Globalization policy. Therefore, it became necessary to separate the Government's policy wing from its operations wing. The Government of India corporatised the operations wing of DoT on 01 October 2000 and named it as Bharat Sanchar Nigam Limited (BSNL). Many private operators, such as Reliance India Mobile, Tata Telecom, Vodafone, BPL, Bharti, Idea etc., successfully entered the high potential Indian telecom market.

Liberalisation of Telcommunications in India

The Indian government was composed of many factions (parties) which had different ideologies. Some of them were willing to throw open the market to foreign players (the centrists) and others wanted the government to regulate infrastructure and restrict the involvement of foreign players. Due to this political background it was very difficult to bring about liberalization in telecommunications. When a bill was in parliament a majority vote had to be passed, and such a majority was difficult to obtain, given to the number of parties having different ideologies. Liberalization started in 1981 when Prime Minister Indira Gandhi signed contracts with Alcatel CIT of France to merge with the state owned Telecom Company (ITI), in an effort to set up 5,000,000 lines per year.

But soon the policy was let down because of political opposition. She invited Sam Pitroda a US based NRI to set up a Centre for Development of Telematics (C-DOT), however the plan failed due to political reasons. During this period, after the assassination of Indira Gandhi, under the leadership of Rajiv Gandhi, many public sector organizations were set up like the Department of Telecommunications (DoT), VSNL and MTNL. Many technological developments took place in this regime but still foreign players were not allowed to participate in the telecommunications business.

The demand for telephones was ever increasing. It was during this period that the P.N Rao led government introduced the national telecommunications policy [NTP] in 1994 which brought changes in the following areas: ownership, service and regulation of telecommunications infrastructure. They were also successful in establishing joint ventures between state owned telecom companies and international players. But still complete ownership of facilities was restricted only to the government owned organizations. Foreign firms were eligible to 49% of the total stake. The multi-nationals were just involved in technology transfer, and not policy making.

During this period, the World Bank and ITU had advised the Indian Government to liberalize long distance services in order to release the monopoly of the state owned DoT and VSNL; and to enable competition in the long distance carrier business which would help reduce tariff's and better the economy of the country. The Rao run government instead liberalized the local services, taking the opposite political parties into confidence and assuring foreign involvement in the long distance business after 5 years. The country was divided into 20 telecommunication circles for basic telephony and 18 circles for mobile services. These circles were divided into category A, B and C depending on the value of the revenue in each circle. The government threw open the bids to one private company per circle along with government owned DoT per circle. For cellular service two service providers were allowed per circle and a 15 years license was given to each provider. During all these improvements, the government did face oppositions from ITI, DoT, MTNL, VSNL and other labour unions, but they managed to keep away from all the hurdles.

After 1995 the government set up TRAI (Telecom Regulatory Authority of India) which reduced the interference of Government in deciding tariffs and policy making. The DoT opposed this.

The political powers changed in 1999 and the new government under the leadership of Atal Bihari Vajpayee was more pro-reforms and introduced better liberalization policies. They split DoT in two-one policy maker and the other service provider (DTS) which was later renamed as BSNL. The proposal of raising the stake of foreign investors from 49% to 74% was rejected by the opposite political party and leftist thinkers. Domestic business groups wanted the government to privatize VSNL. Finally in April 2002, the government decided to cut its stake of 53% to 26% in VSNL and to throw it open for sale to private enterprises. TATA finally took 25% stake in VSNL.

This was a gateway to many foreign investors to get entry into the Indian Telecom Markets. After March 2000, the government became more liberal in making policies and issuing licenses to private operators. The government further reduced license fees for cellular service providers and increased the allowable stake to 74% for foreign companies. Because of all these factors, the service fees finally reduced and the call costs were cut greatly enabling every common middle class family in India to afford a cell phone.

Growth of Mobile Technology

India has become one of the fastest-growing mobile markets in the world. The mobile services were commercially launched in August 1995 in India. In the initial 5–6 years the average monthly subscribers additions were around 0.05 to 0.1 million only and the total mobile subscribers base in December 2002 stood at 10.5 millions. However, after the number of proactive initiatives taken by regulator and licensor, the monthly mobile subscriber additions increased to around 2 million per month in the year 2003-04 and 2004-05.

Although mobile telephones followed the New Telecom Policy 1994, growth was tardy in the early years because of the high price of hand sets as well as the high tariff structure of mobile telephones. The New Telecom Policy in 1999, the industry heralded several pro consumer initiatives. Mobile subscriber additions started picking up.

The number of mobile phones added throughout the country in 2003 was 16 million, followed by 22 million in 2004, 32 million in 2005 and 65 million in 2006. As of January 2009, total mobile phone subscribers numbered 362 million, having added 15 million that month alone. India ranks second in mobile phone usage to China, with 472 million users as of September 2009.

India has opted for the use of both the GSM (global system for mobile communications) and CDMA (code-division multiple access) technologies in the mobile sector. In addition to landline and mobile phones, some of the companies also provide the WLL service.

The mobile tariffs in India have also become lowest in the world. A new mobile connection can be activated with a monthly commitment of US$0.15 only. In 2005 alone 32 million handsets were sold in India. The data reveals the real potential for growth of the Indian mobile market.

In March 2008 the total GSM and CDMA mobile subscriber base in the country was 375 million, which represented a nearly 50% growth when compared with previous year.

In April 2008 the Indian Department of Telecom (DoT) has directed all mobile phone service users to disconnect the usage of unbranded Chinese mobile phones that do not have International Mobile Equipment Identity (IMEI) numbers, because they pose a serious security risk to the country. Mobile network operators therefore planned to suspend the usage of around 30 million mobile phones (about 8 % of all mobiles in the country) by 30 April.

Revenue and Growth

The total revenue in the telecom service sector was Rs. 86,720 crore in 2005-06 as against Rs. 71, 674 crore in 2004-2005, registering a growth of 21%. The total investment in the telecom services sector reached Rs. 200,660 crore in 2005-06, up from Rs. 178,831 crore in the previous fiscal.

Telecommunication is the lifeline of the rapidly growing Information Technology industry. Internet subscriber base has risen to 6.94 million in 2005-2006. Out of this 1.35 million were broadband connections. More than a billion people use the internet globally.

Under the Bharat Nirman Programme, the Government of India will ensure that 66,822 revenue villages in the country, which have not yet been provided with a Village Public Telephone (VPT), will be connected. However doubts have been raised about what it would mean for the poor in the country.

It is difficult to ascertain fully the employment potential of the telecom sector but the enormity of the opportunities can be gauged from the fact that there were 3.7 million Public Call Offices in December 2005 up from 2.3 million in December 2004.

The value added services (VAS) market within the mobile industry in India has the potential to grow from $500 million in 2006 to a whopping $10 billion by 2009.

Telephone

On landlines, intra circle calls are considered local calls while inter circle are considered long distance calls. Currently Government is working to integrate the whole country in one telecom circle. For long distance calls, you dial the area code prefixed with a zero (e.g. For calling Delhi, you would dial 011-XXXX XXXX). For international calls, you would dial "00" and the country code+area code+number. The country code for India is 91.

Until recently, only the PSU's BSNL and MTNL were allowed to provide Basic Phone Service through copper wires in India. MTNL is operating in Delhi and Mumbai only and all other parts are covered by BSNL. However private operators have now entered the fray, although their focus is largely on the cellular business which is growing rapidly.

- Telephony Subscribers (Wireless and Landline): 525.85 million (Oct. 2009)
- Cellphones: 488.4 million (Oct. 2009)
- Land Lines: 37.25 million (Oct. 2009)
- Yearly Cellphone Addition: 113.26 million (2007)
- Monthly Cellphone Addition: 16.67 million (Oct. 2009)
- Teledensity: 44.85% (Oct. 2009)
- Projected teledensity: 626 million, 46% of population by 2010.

Internet

The number of broadband connections in India have seen a continuous growth since the beginning of 2006. At the end of August 2008, total broadband connections in the country have reached 4.73 million.

BSNL, Sify, MTNL, STPI, Airtel, Netcom, Reliance Communications and Hathway are some of the major ISPs in India. TRAI has defined broadband as 256 kbit/s or higher. However, many ISPs advertise their service as broadband but don't offer the suggested speeds. Broadband in India is more expensive as compared to Western Europe/United Kingdom and United States.

After economic liberalization in 1992, many private ISPs have entered the market, many with their own local loop and gateway infrastructures. The telecom services market is regulated by TRAI. ADSL providers include:

- Tata Communications Ltd. (VSNL)
- MTNL/BSNL
- Bharti Telecom (Airtel, Bharti Televentures)
- Reliance Infocomm.

Because of the increase in ISPs and the quality of service Qos, It became cheaper to call India from around the world. Many Indians today, studying or living all around the world, are using calling cards to India to speak with their families back home. It used to be much more expensive prior to 2002.

Broadband

The current definition of Broadband in India is speeds of 256 kbit/s. TRAI on July 2009 has recommened raising this limit to 2 Mbps. As of September 2009, India has 7.21 million broadband users. In the fixed line arena, BSNL and MTNL are the incumbents in their respective areas of operation and continue to enjoy the dominant service provider status in the domain of fixed line services. For example BSNL controls 79% of fixed line share in the country.

On the other hand, in the mobile telephony space, Airtel controls 21.4% subscriber base followed by Reliance with 20.3%, BSNL with 18.6%, Vodafone with 14.7% subscriber base (as per June 2005 data).

Airtel and BSNL have launched 8 Mbit/s & Reliance Communication offers 10 Mb/s broadband internet services in selected areas recently. For home users, the maximum speed for unlimited downloads is 2 Mbit/s, available for USD 60 (roughly, without taxes) per month.

Broadcasting

In India, only the government owned *Doordarshan* (*Door* = Distant= Tele, *Darshan* = Vision) is allowed to broadcast terrestrial television signals. It initially had one major National channel (DD National) and a Metro channel in some of the larger cities (also known as DD Metro).

Satellite/Cable television took off during the first Gulf War with CNN. There are no regulations against ownership of satellite dish antennas, or operation of cable television systems, which led to an explosion of viewership and channels, led by the Star TV group and Zee TV. Initially restricted to music and entertainment channels, viewership grew, giving rise to several channels in regional languages and many in the national language, Hindi. The main news channels available were CNN and BBC World. In the late 1990s, many current affairs and news channels sprouted, becoming immensely popular because of the alternative viewpoint they offered compared to Doordarshan. Some of the notable ones are Aaj Tak (means *Till Today*, run by the India Today group) and Star News, initially run by the NDTV group and their lead anchor, Prannoy Roy (NDTV now has its own channels, NDTV 24x7, NDTV Profit, NDTV India and NDTV Imagine). New Delhi Television.

Adherence of Indian News Channels to Cardinal Principles of Broadcasting

In the current liberalized environment that is characterized by information and knowledge base, the media, particularly the satellite television news channels, is a very powerful medium that plays a significant role in shaping public opinions and beliefs, and disseminating correct information and knowledge with a huge responsibility on their shoulders.

Such dissemination of news, views, and other information has far-reaching affects on societies, businesses, and governments. At the same time, today, the electronic media attracts the best talent in the country. When talented people work in such an industry, society expects them to act in a more accountable manner and provide it with those news stories that will increase their knowledge, their sources of information, and inspire them to inculcate a feeling of responsibility toward society.

It is said that Indian viewers now spend more time watching news than reading news, as TV news channels in India have been competing with each other for more viewership. They have been targeting specific viewers by producing interactive and sensational types of news programs for vying for public attention and ultimately to improve their television rating points (T.R.P.). However, there has been severe public criticism of their programs resulting in a decline in the confidence level of the public. Some recent public opinion surveys reveal that the Indian news channels often resort to bias reporting, create insensitivity, contain inaccuracies, promote sensationalism and trivialization in news content, have conflicts of interest and a lack of depthlessness in their news and views stories. Furthermore, they are also criticized that "the channels tend to miss out on important stories in this scramble for eyeballs. 'Hardly 25 percent of national news bulletins are about health, education, development, welfare, environment, etc.'"

It is also seen that most of these TV news channels have been resorting to Page 3 type reporting, which reflects negatively in the minds of Indian youth despite the fact that every channel, whether Star News, Zee News, NDTV or even Aaj Tak, often claims that it is a socially responsible news channels.

Also, for example, Zee News on its Web site claims that it "has dared to walk a different path to bring the truth out even if it means staying away from hype and trivial sensationalism." The selection and type of news dissemination clearly indicates declining accountability on their part. Also, some of the news content on Star News and Zee News seems to be objectionable.

Furthermore, in a recently concluded study, S. Rao and N. S. Johal found that media ethics is not a topic being widely discussed in Indian newsrooms and TV stations. Marketing pressures, the "tabloidization" of news, and management and economic pressures are affecting journalism ethics and issues such as accountability, independence, and conflict of interests (2006). From the above, it seems that these news channels perhaps lack a definite focus and may have diverged from the cardinal principles of broadcasting to which they should be adhering.

It also seems that many of the news channels by and large are working on old strategy of creating one package for different time bands. Consequently, they seem to be lacking in introducing innovative news programs. According to one commentator: "The amount of real news they give to the viewers out of their 24 hours of constant feeding is very less. With 24 hours to fill in and rat race of improving own T.R.P. among hundreds of other channels, news channels are stooping to any level to produce what they call the 'news'" and none of them truly seem to be delivering news (Vivek 2006). Often they depend on Bollywood stars for their survival.

For example, some news channels have been overburdened with news related to celebrities such as Amitabh Bachchan, Aiswarya Rai, Abhishek Bachchan, Amar Singh, and Sharukh Khan in order to woo their viewers and improve its T.R.P. The question would be whether this stardom makes news every day and night. This is all trivia and fluff and it looks as though some of the news channels are the main mouthpiece for rich and famous people.

This clearly reflects that gradual privatization and deregulation have resulted in increased entertainment-driven rather than public service oriented news channels in India. In other words, rather than being a news channel, they are trying to become wholesome entertainment channels even though there are other channels for this purpose. In order to survive the intense competition in this field, they often go in for sensationalism; for example, conducting sting operations in the cash-for-question scandal and in exposing corruption among M.P.'s in selecting the projects for a local area development scheme.

It also seems that Indian TV news channels are yet to completely mature when it comes to content. Most of the channels have been resorting to trivialization of news, which is a serious issue. For example, some of the news channels were severely criticized for blowing up things with their exclusive programs on for example the 2006 Delhi sealing drive. Other examples include the episode of Rakhi and Mika, or the woman in Orissa who fell in love with a snake and decided to get married to it, etc.

Data shows that the viewer stays with a channel only if it presents it with depth and responsibility and follows the story to its logical conclusion. Bhaswati Ghosh argues that "whether it be the case of a Hindi film actor being abused in the middle of the night by a fellow actor or the episode of a girl calling the police on her wedding day to arrest her dowry-demanding husband, the channels waste no time to latch on to such spicy topics and dish out soap-opera style stories on them. Within no time, a timid, conforming, submissive girl was turned into a national icon, the very symbol of 21st century womanhood and the channels even encouraged viewers to send congratulatory S.M.S.'s to her through their network".

Another criticism against news channels is their anchor-centric character. "Almost all the channels seem to be obsessed with the idea of putting glamour and style ahead of content and credibility.... Indian anchors seem to be completely neglectful of the need to sharpen their journalistic skills" (2003). Their diction and pronunciation is also of concern to viewers. On the other hand, some experts argue that the "BBC and CNN ... are always careful about choosing their anchors, who in turn are mostly attuned to current happenings, their backgrounds, and future impacts".

The Cardinal Principles of Broadcasting and Objectives of the Survey

The cardinal principles of broadcasting were identified by Sir Alan Hulme at the first General Assembly of Asia Pacific Broadcasting Union in 1964 and endorsed by the Fourth Asian Broadcasting Conference to be followed by the electronic media. In 1999, Sir William Deane in his inaugural speech in the Asia Pacific Broadcasting Union General Assembly stated that these principles not only remain valid today, they have become immeasurably more important for electronic media.

The cardinal principles included in this study: (1) to ensure the objective presentation of news and fair and unbiased comments; (2) to promote the advancement of education and culture; (3) to provide programs for the young, which, by variety and content, will inculcate the principles of good citizenship; (4) to promote communal harmony, religious tolerance and international understanding; (5) to treat controversial public issues in an impartial and dispassionate manner; and (6) to respect human rights and dignity.

Motivated by criticism and concern about news channels, a survey was targeted to non-resident Indians (N.R.I.'s) living in the Persian Gulf region to understand their perceptions on the extent to which satellite Indian TV news channels have been adhering to the above cardinal principles of broadcasting. Furthermore, the survey also aims to examine which TV news channels the N.R.I.'s consider their favourite and whether these TV news channels have been promoting news, views, and other programs related to N.R.I.'s. The basic intention behind this survey is to generate more interest and awareness among Persian Gulf-based N.R.I.'s toward issues and news originating in their homeland and elsewhere so that they remain well informed about happenings in India. Also, to elicit suggestions, and to determine whether the TV news channels need to be regulated in order to make them more accountable to society.

N.R.I.'s in the Persian Gulf Region

N.R.I.'s living in the Persian Gulf region have been playing a key role in its economic transformation as well as in the economic transformation of India. They send about $6 billion annually to India by way of remittances. They are unique in the sense that they will not be naturalized in this region and ultimately will return to their homeland. Furthermore, they not only show relatively higher current ownership of both physical and financial assets in India, but are also the ones who have a relatively higher propensity to make further investments in shares and deposits in India.

About 45.9 percent of them live in Saudi Arabia, followed by the United Arab Emirates with 27.5 percent. A majority of them are labourers who work in different industries, particularly in the construction sector. The satellite Indian TV news channels are very important for them, as they are kept informed of current events and happenings in India. To subscribe to TV channels, they pay a handsome fee ranging from 25,000 to 35,000 Indian rupees annually. Therefore, they also expect that Indian news channels should produce news, views, and other programs related to them from the Persian Gulf region.

Methodology

The survey follows an online convenient random survey technique. The participants were selected randomly from a number of sources whose e-mail addresses were publicly available; for example, from Indiagrid.com, various Web sites related to N.R.I.'s, associations of N.R.I.'s in Gulf countries, social clubs, Indian schools, company Web sites, etc. In such a survey, it is not possible to establish a universe for the respondents. A total of 1,291 e-mails, with an attached copy of the questionnaire, were sent out to N.R.I.'s in six countries: Bahrain, United Arab Emirates, Saudi Arabia, Qatar, Kuwait, and Oman. When requested by some respondents, copies of the questionnaires were also sent by fax.

The survey was conducted with the help of a questionnaire. The questionnaire contained demographic information: the frequency of watching news channels, favourite channel(s), whether these news channels offered programs on N.R.I.'s, whether they adhered to the six cardinal principles of broadcasting, etc. In an open-end question, comments and suggestions were also elicited. The six satellite TV news channels, both Hindi and English—NDTV, Star News, Zee News, Aaj Tak, Channel 7, and Sahara News—were included in the study.

The questionnaire was pre-tested with 10 people from three countries and after obtaining their feedback, the questionnaire was improved. The responses from these people were excluded from the final responses.

Out of 1,291 questionnaires sent out, 274 replies were received back. However, the usable questionnaires were only 222 (17.2 percent). Some respondents did not provide personal information and 14 respondents stated that they were no longer working in Persian Gulf and were resident in India now. Therefore, such responses were dropped from the final analysis. In order to increase the response rate, about 42 percent of the N.R.I.'s were sent reminders three weeks after the first e-mails were sent to them.

Results and Discussions

It is clear that most of the respondents were highly qualified as 109 (49.1 percent) of them had postgraduate and higher qualifications. Moreover, 40.2 percent of respondents were executives and managers who may have a better understanding of the news and views for common purposes. Many of them were academicians and housewives. About 58.6 percent had been living in this region for more than 10 years. The respondents were a mix of young and older people.

Frequency of Watching and Favourite News Channels

Furthermore, it seems that NDTV is the favourite news channel among the N.R.I.'s in the Persian Gulf region. Whereas, only 49 percent of them stated that Star News is their highly favourite or favourite channel. It seems that females were more inclined to watch Star News as 71 percent of them considered it their favourite news channel. Does it mean that females are more interested in watching Bollywood *masala* type news? ["Masala" is Hindi for "spices."] On the other hand, it appears that professionals (executives/managers) and academicians were more inclined to watch NDTV. Many of them stated that NDTV is for a matured audience. Furthermore, though only 55 respondents in the sample stated that they watch Aaj Tak, about 70 percent of them also considered this channel as their favourite. This may not be surprising because in the past, surveys by A.C. Nielsen, Cyber-Media Research, and others (Exchange4media.com 2003) reveal that viewers in India perceived Aaj Tak as the most popular Hindi news channel. Only 31.83 percent of respondents said Zee News was their favourite channel. However, more than 50 percent of them were neutral on this account.

About 17.9 percent of the respondents stated that Zee News was their least favourite channel and more than 13 percent stated so for Star News.

Adherence to the Cardinal Principles of Broadcasting

The main objective of this survey was to examine the perceptions of Persian Gulf-based N.R.I.'s on the extent to which Indian TV news channels adhere to the six principles of broadcasting. Again, these are in part: (1) "promoting the advancement of education and culture"; (2) "ensuring the objective presentation of news and fair and unbiased comment"; (3) "providing programs for the young, which, by variety and content, will inculcate the principles of good citizenship"; and (4) "respecting human rights and dignity." Over 81 percent of the respondents stated support for these principles in this survey.

Therefore, the perceptions of Persian Gulf-based N.R.I.'s reflect that NDTV by working various strategies and offering a variety of news programs with vastly experienced presenters and hosts, a semblance of professionalism, etc., to a large extent, is adhering to the above principles. A few respondents stated that some of its programs seem to be popular like "Walk the Talk," "The Big Fight," "We the People," etc. At the same time, it also seems that its hosts try their best to provide down-to-earth news sensibly.

On the other hand, the survey also shows that TV news channels in India seem to have failed to deal with the issue of "treating controversial public issues in an impartial and dispassionate manner." The respondents ranked this principle among the lowest in the order. Star News and Zee News received the lowest mean scores on this principle. It also seems that TV news channels are often biased in favour of popular interest news; for example, when we turn to any news channel, the same story is making the rounds or keeps being repeated. For instance, when Sanjay Dutta, a film actor, was relieved by the court, the same story was repeated for several days by these news channels.

Furthermore, none of them seems to be successful in achieving the principle of "promoting communal harmony, religious tolerance, and international understanding." Zee News scored the lowest mean (2.76) on this principle. The respondents seem to have perceived that the news channels have fewer programs for promoting communal harmony, religious tolerance, and international understanding. "The news channels should have focused more on these issues as the present times are very critical especially where all sorts of extremism is taking roots, especially religious," commented a female respondent from Dubai.

There were some sharp comments that news channels strongly lack programs on the development of Indian youth and women's education. Three respondents remarked that Star News deals less on the economic and social issues and concentrates more on political and Bollywood personalities.

It seems that most of the news channels' programs are still local and national, as they do not have a global reach yet. The news channels hardly cover more segment-specific news capsules such as I.T., B.P.O., global warming, etc. The respondents also stated that more international coverage, especially from the Middle East region, is required.

A country-wise analysis of responses shows that there were not many significant differences in the perceptions of the respondents. The significant difference was observed only in respect of "providing programs for the young, which, by variety and content, will inculcate the principles of good citizenship" for Star News ($F=2.62$; $p<0.005$).

Furthermore, there were also not many significant differences in the results when analysed by gender. The only significant difference was found in respect to "promoting the advancement of education and culture" for Zee News (t-test=2.55; $p<0.05$) and in respect to "promoting the advancement of education and culture" for Aaj Tak (t-test=2.93; $p<0.01$).

Significant differences in perceptions were found when results were analysed by N.R.I. status, profession, education, and age. This indicates that the degree of their perceptions differ considerably across the news channels, particularly for NDTV, Star News, and Zee News, in adhering to various principles of broadcasting.

The significant differences were particularly observed for "ensuring the objective presentation of news and fair and unbiased comment," "promoting the advancement of education and culture," "promoting communal harmony, religious tolerance, and international understanding," and "treating controversial public issues in an impartial and dispassionate manner."

The Four C's of Indian TV News Channels and 'Tabloidization,' Sensationalization and Trivialization of News Content

In an open-ended question, several respondents provided comments and suggestions on TV news channels. From a review of these comments and suggestions, it seems that the satellite TV news channels in India follow a combination of current news, feature news, and feature stories, but these mainly concentrate on four C's, i.e., corruption, criminals, celebrities, and cricket. A fifth C may also be added, namely "customs-related-superstitions," as some of them stated that the news channels, particularly Zee News and Star News, also show daily programs related to superstitions prevalent in society.

It is a reflection of presenting stereotyped news and analysis to viewers. Furthermore, two respondents from Bahrain also commented that the news content had more news and views about metropolitan cities and hardly any news coverage from rural India.

News coverage is more focused on Bollywood *masala* than on the happenings with the common people in the country. Therefore, the quantity of news reporting is not necessarily translated into quality.

Many times, the news channels including NDTV dramatize news stories. Sometimes the news stories are trivial but are treated as international news or breaking news. Very often, the channels seem unable to distinguish between breaking news and common news. For breaking news, they should highlight events that are of national and international importance. The sensationalization, trivialization, and "tabloidization" of news stories distort its intellectual characteristics, which may lead to less accurate and biased reporting.

Such news stories are usually seen on lean news days. In this regard, one general manager of a leading company in the region argued: "What we listen to and see on TV news channels influences our thought processes. Hence, we should have programs that will teach and promote open, free, clean, clear, unbiased thinking. If we don't look at things in clear mind for what it is, we will not see the thing as it actually is." Also, two respondents commented that news analysis on Star News lacks quality and needs rethinking on their part. It seems that the program on "Desh Videsh/National Reporter" of Star News appeals to respondents.

At the same time, two respondents were glad to see that Indian news channels actively provided news coverage on the duties of the judiciary in India, for example, for the cases of Jessica Lal, and Nitish Kataria. One respondent suggested: "A portion of airtime should be dedicated for socially responsible awareness in the areas of education, health, hygiene, environment, communal harmony, national pride, etc.

Graphic videos of violence, killings, crimes/news related to communal tensions, etc., should be presented in a more mature manner." Another respondent from Bahrain who happens to be an editor argued, "The news channels in India must develop a more mature approach while presenting news reports so that viewers are able to get a broader picture of the news report." Respondents were also very critical about the presentation of news by some newsreaders on these channels.

Two senior executives from a big organization were least satisfied with the way the news is read by the newsreaders. They strongly suggested that their diction and pronunciation must be improved. Often they commit glaring mistakes in pronouncing even common words. Several of them suggested that "news channels should employ experienced journalists who know what questions to ask instead of hiring youngsters simply because they look presentable."

Another respondent from Oman commented: "the language and body language of presenters [needs] to be more controlled and composed. Language seems to be usually closer to 'over exaggeration' and body language usually is hyper. A common code of conduct should be developed by the news channels themselves."

At the same time, they should be "more proactive and investigative, and should stick to responsible reporting. Many news channels, in most cases, have been presently following a drop the 'report and forget' policy. They should keep reporting till the logical outcome is achieved/reached." On many occasions, it is also seen that when the TV news camera is focused on a particular event, the degree of hyperactivity of the presenter is so high it looks as if the TV news channels have put the whole world in their pocket.

Programs for N.R.I.'s

The respondents also addressed a question on which news channels cover the news, views, and other programs related to N.R.I.'s. Surprisingly, a majority of them stated that none of the news channels really cover news about N.R.I.'s.

About 24 percent of respondents suggested that all channels should have at least some programs that inform N.R.I.'s about various facilities on savings, investments, banking, real estate, etc. in India. It is their social and moral responsibility to inform N.R.I.'s about education courses in India, and the facilities and latest trends in education in India for their children.

One respondent from Kuwait was critical about news channels. She stated that "news on underworld, e.g., Dawood [underworld don Dawood Ibrahim], is not the news for N.R.I.'s in the Gulf. These news channels must develop programs about Indian labourers' working and living conditions in the Gulf. Unfortunately, they do not give any good and realistic news about them."

Many of them argued that they pay subscription fees between 20,000 and 35,000 Indian rupees annually for the news and other channels, which is a substantial amount compared to what their counterparts in India pay. Still these news channels do not cover any news related to N.R.I.'s. There were suggestions that the government of India should start an exclusive channel devoted to N.R.I.'s.

Regulating the News Channels

Another question asked to the respondents was whether the government of India should bring or modify existing laws to regulate TV news channels in the country. Those who were against bringing regulation argued that the regulation would impair the innovation and integration of programs of news channels.

One prominent N.R.I. who held a very senior position in India and is now in Oman commented, "Not necessarily; it is just these channels have their roots established. With the competitions existing in the market, they have to remain accountable to the public, whether laws exist or not. They will continue to improve their standards and quality. Imposing them through statute will only curb their innovativeness and integrated functioning."

Furthermore, there were statistically significant differences among the respondents when the responses were analysed by profession ($p<0.01$ level), by N.R.I. status ($p<0.01$ level), and by age group ($p<0.01$).

Executives and managers were more in favour of regulating the news channels. At the same time, respondents who had been staying for a longer period in the Persian Gulf region and were older were also in favour of regulation.

Other suggestions were as follows:

- "Realize that investigative journalism involves more than just string operations."
- "The focus on revenues from advertisement should be shifted to news and bringing more news to the doorsteps of the public."
- "The coverage of political news should not be restricted to the mainstream political parties alone."
- "Apart from politics, films, and sports, the coverage should be extended to developments in the fields of art, culture, science, literature, etc. since they also make news."
- "The so-called reality shows peeping into private lives of individuals (even ordinary folks) is scandalous, is not journalism, and should be discouraged, if not altogether banned."

- "The channels need advertisement revenue—but not at the cost of interruption every three to five minutes. In one hour, they can have 30 minutes uninterrupted coverage, 10 minutes advertisements run, and 20 minutes analysis. This is just an example. News has to be continuous with maximum one break for few seconds."
- "The technical team must be equipped with the state of the art and must support the newsreaders. In certain live programs, we invariably see the audio signals of anchors at various cities or locations not reaching, whereas the video is visible (or vice versa)."
- "The response from the anchors must be spontaneous and not wait for the readers' signals to reach them. The time gap for their response is irritating."
- "The quality of impartial reporting must be enhanced."
- "At no time should they telecast scenes that can only be viewed with people of good heart conditions."
- "The compassionate feelings of the affected persons must be honored. The "flash" or "breaking news" items must be of some standard and national importance and not routine items."
- "Avoid sensationalism at all costs."
- "Curb on vulgar and violence clippings."
- "More focus on positive news stories and more focus on younger generation issues."
- "Where exactly we are failing and to highlight regularly?"
- "News on women's education and development should be focused more. These are news channels and not entertainment channels. They should cut down Bollywood related programs, which do not offer any career development values to us."
- "Stop making socially undesirable characters as national heroes. Less exaggeration or avoid undue importance given to politicians/political drama."

Conclusions and Implications

Non-resident Indians while staying abroad can update themselves about all the happenings in their motherland when they have access to satellite Indian TV news channels. The perceptions of N.R.I.'s from the Persian Gulf region show that the major news channels need to rethink their current program strategies. They believe that, baring NDTV, TV news channels by and large have not been strictly adhering to the cardinal principles of broadcasting. Consequently, they often fall into the vicious circle of providing news stories that may be tabloid, sensational, trivial, and stereotypical, not necessarily reflecting dynamism, and innovation.

These characteristics may make their news and views program biased and less accurate. NDTV seems to be the only channel that has been following these cardinal principles to a large extent. However, Indian news channels seem to have failed in dealing with the issue of "treating controversial public issues in an impartial and dispassionate manner." As TV news channels in India currently are considered to be entertainment-driven rather than public service oriented, perhaps they need to bring some reforms to their news programs, culture, and ethics that give a clear reflection on adhering to the cardinal principles of broadcasting.

Every channel may also need to do an extensive research on different concepts and different themes to attract more viewers. Any modifications to the existing regulations that would make them more accountable to the public but without impairing their innovation and working freedom would be welcomed.

They should resort to a fair commercial approach in their programs, which is healthy, innovative, and social-oriented. They should cut down on balloon-filling news and the overdose of cinema, fashion shows, and Page 3 reporting, etc.

The news channels really need worthy investment to derive qualitatively better coverage and interpretation of both socially relevant issues as well as scientific and educational issues.

They should expand their reporting boundaries beyond the happenings in Bollywood and political circles and should cover unwanted and hidden corners of society and the world. As Nihal Singh, the well-known journalist, argued in an article, "It is time for Indian television to shape up and rank high in world ratings".

The news channels should start some news coverage programs for N.R.I.'s, say, three hours on a weekly basis. Alternatively, the government of India should start a separate TV channel exclusively meant to benefit N.R.I.'s as they have been playing a significant role in the economic development of the country.

Next Generation Networks

In the Next Generation Networks, multiple access networks can connect customers to a core network based on IP technology. These access networks include fibre optics or coaxial cable networks connected to fixed locations or customers connected through wi-fi as well as to 3G networks connected to mobile users.

As a result, in the future, it would be impossible to identify whether the next generation network is a fixed or mobile network and the wireless access broadband would be used both for fixed and mobile services. It would then be futile to differentiate between fixed and mobile networks– both fixed and mobile users will access services through a single core network.

Indian telecom networks are not so intensive as developed country's telecom networks and India's teledensity is low only in rural areas. 670,000 route kilometres (419,000 miles) of optical fibres has been laid in India by the major operators, even in remote areas and the process continues.

BSNL alone, has laid optical fibre to 30,000 Telephone Exchanges out of their 36 Exchanges. Keeping in mind the viability of providing services in rural areas, an attractive solution appears to be one which offers multiple service facility at low costs.

A rural network based on the extensive optical fibre network, using Internet Protocol and offering a variety of services and the availability of open platforms for service development, viz. the Next Generation Network, appears to be an attractive proposition. Fibre network can be easily converted to Next Generation network and then used for delivering multiple services at cheap cost.

International

- Nine satellite earth stations-8 Intelsat (Indian Ocean) and 1 Inmarsat (Indian Ocean region).
- Nine gateway exchanges operating from Mumbai, New Delhi, Kolkata, Chennai, Jalandhar, Kanpur, Gandhinagar, Hyderabad and Ernakulam.

Submarine Cables

- LOCOM linking Chennai to Penang, Malaysia
- India-UAEcable linking Mumbai to Al Fujayrah, UAE.
- SEA-ME-WE 2, SEA-ME-WE 3, SEA-ME-WE 4-(South East Asia-Middle East-Western Europe) with landing sites at Cochin and Mumbai.
- Fiber-Optic Link Around the Globe (FLAG) with a landing site at Mumbai (2000).

The World of Spoken Word

The Spoken Word: The Base for Writing and Reading

Consciously or unconsciously, we recognize that language has rules and infer those rules. We learn rules of sentence structure, such as how to use pronouns to replace noun phrases or the order of adjectives before a noun. We learn social aspects of language usage. such as when to use slang and when not to. We learn the need to apply prior knowledge and experience when trying to make sense of utterances. We learn that the goal is not to understand words,*per se*, so much as to understand the deas behind the words.

Finally, our model of spoken communication serves as a tool for understanding the written language.

Reading and the Spoken Language

The language we learned first, the spoken language, remains our base throughout life. We use the model of spoken communication as the basis for much of our inferences when we read.

As readers, we imagine the written language to be a transcription of speech. We draw on this model when we imagine ourselves talking to someone as we write, or when we talk about what an author "has to say" in an article. When we run into trouble reading, we sound out words and read sentences aloud. When discussing the spoken word, we refer to a speaker's tone of voice. Is he or she angry? Ironic? Or perhaps serious? If the language is jarring, we say the tone is harsh. In doing so, we infer emotions on the part of the author.

Ultimately, the underlying reason for relying on speech as a model for writing may actually lie in the nature of human understanding.

The core of psychological understanding revolves around the notion of motive—desire, want, wish, reason. We understand an action when we know what motivated it. The motives for action are usually clear, since action itself usually indicates the motive that prompts it. Why am I paying money to the cashier in a supermarket?

So that I can buy food and eventually eat it. We generally act in order to fulfil our manifest wishes. Sometimes the motives for action can be obscure, as when you see me searching frantically in a drawer and don't know that I left a lot of money in there and now can't find it. Motives are internal mental states that cause action and that make sense of actions; action is seen as rational in the light of motives that lead to it. We apply this reasoning to both the motivation for the ideas of a text as well as to the author's motive for writing that text.

Readers, just as listeners, infer intent, motive, purpose, tone, mood, and point of view as a way of making sense of a text. We claim to understand a text when we can identify a clear purpose and intent. We think beyond the words of the text to what might make sense in terms of a communication between specific people in a specific situation.

Writing to an Audience

Writing, like speaking, is concerned with communicating specific thoughts or information to a specified audience. To be understood, we must take into account the prior knowledge of our audience. To be effective, we must recognize issues of power or prestige that our readers have at stake and why they might not initially accept our arguments. We should look at writing not only as a matter of what to say, but also as a matter of what to do.

- how to interest our readers,
- how to educate them, and
- how to convince them.

Just as our readers will image an author behind our text, so we as writers must imagine an audience and be sensitive to the same needs and social conventions that we would consider in face-to-face speech.

What Did the Author Really Mean?

Viewing texts within the model of spoken language is a useful technique, but it is not without its dangers. On the face of it, the author of a text is a figment of the reader's imagination, a mental image constructed from prior knowledge of the real-life author (accurate or not) and the remarks on the page.

Questions about the real author and his or her purpose in writing a particular text can be answered only by talking with the living author. Racists can write non-racist texts and vice versa. Even then we cannot be entirely sure what an author truly intended. An author might not be forthcoming about his or her purpose. And whatever the author's intentions, he or she may not have successfully communicated that intended meaning within the text.

When we ask what an author meant, our reference to "the author" is really a metaphor for the text: what might the text mean? Inferring an author can be a useful tool for making sense of remarks within a text, but we must not make the jump from analysis of evidence within the text to speculation about a person who is not present. While we cannot know what an author intended, we can try to figure out what meaning makes the most sense given all we know from the evidence of the text, about the author and the situation at the time, and the social context.

Readers must exert the same caution when discussing the audience of a text as they do when discussing the author. Readers may infer an audience to whom they imagine a text might appeal. As with the notion of the author above, the notion of an audience for a text is essentially a tool for describing and explaining features of a text. It may or may not actually indicate people for whom the text might have been, intended.

Television Sector in India

The number of private satellite TV channels has grown astronomically over the years, from 1 TV channel in 2000 to 273 TV channels in 2007 (till 31.12.2007).

The number of non-news & current affairs TV channels has grown from 0 to 115 and that of news & current affairs TV channels has grown from 1 to 158.

DTH Service

Direct-To-Home (DTH) Service refers to distribution of multi-channel TV programmes in Ku Band by using a satellite system for providing TV signals direct to subscribers' premises.

DTH provides subscribers the advantage of geographical mobility meaning thereby that once a customer purchases DTH hardware, he/she can continue to use the same unit anywhere in India. DD DIRECT+ is India's first and only Free To Air (FTA) Direct-To-Home Service being provided by Prasar Bharati. Apart from Prasar Bharati-a public service broadcaster, M/s Dish TV India Ltd. M/s Tata Sky Ltd, and M/s Sun Direct TV Pvt. Ltd. M/s Reliance Big TV Pvt. Ltd., M/s Bharti Telemedia Ltd.and M/s. Bharat Business Channel Ltd. have also been granted license for operating DTH service.

The eligibility conditions provide for total foreign equity holding, including FDI/NRI/OCB/FII, in the applicant company not to exceed 49%, and within the foreign equity, the FDI component not to exceed 20%. It also provides that applicant company must have Indian management control with the majority representatives on the Board as well as Chief Executive of the Company being resident Indians.

Radio Sector

During the year, the Cabinet approved the grant of permission to the FM broadcasting companies for creation of subsidiaries, and merger/demerger/amalgamations of companies by way of transfer of shares in partial modification of the policy on expansion of FM Radio Broadcasting services through Private Agencies. Total 241 private FM Channels are operational in 83 cities of the country. A total amount of Rs.1609 crores received by way of licence fees from private FM Channels, including Rs.40.5 crores during the current year. The Government has also conveyed its views on FM Phase III policy to TRAI and sought for its recommendation.

FM Policy Phase-II has been well accepted by all stakeholders, which resulted in huge growth not only in FM radio industry but also in employment opportunity and has also created a demand for FM radio in other cities. Keeping this in mind and to accelerate further growth of FM industry, the Government intends to further expand FM radio to other cities through private agencies under Phase-III.

Satellite Radio

At present M/s Worldspace India Private Ltd, a wholly owned subsidiary of M/s Worldspace Asia Pvt. Ltd. Singapore, is providing these services under an FIPB approval dated 7.12.1998. World Space has been permitted to undertake the following activities-

(i) For setting up of a 100% wholly owned subsidiary for carrying out software programming activities in India in the fields of educational, sports and entertainment software programmes as under:

(a) Sourcing/commissioning/production of digital audio and multimedia software programmes for international and domestic market.

(b) Setting up state-of-art studios using latest equipment.

(c) Providing research, consultancy & other service in related areas.

(ii) To import digital satellite receivers, data adaptors, PC-add-on cards and accessories and sell the same to the distributors/dealers either as customs bonded warehouse sale or on a cash and carry basis for introducing international standard, state-of-the-art audio receivers in India to meet the growing requirement for use of World space systems for different application including education, disaster management and development communications.

(iii) To set up customer care centre in all the major centres.

(iv) To carry out various services to its parent/associates companies in realizing the revenue opportunities arising out of education, information and entertainment and other services of World space Systems like collection of revenue. Usage of revenue collected for activities specified by World space in India.

(v) To establish a call centre and services.

Community Radio

Radio as a communication medium plays an important role in the nation's sociocultural, political and economic development. Community radio, as distinct from public service broadcasting, serves to bring small communities together, focuses on the common man's day-to-day concerns and helps in realising local aspirations. In a number of countries, community radio has played an important role in informing and empowering people, especially the poor and vulnerable groups and gives a voice to the voiceless.

The Policy on Community Radio was liberalized during the year 2008 to bring in the civil society and voluntary organizations working not for profit also under its ambit. Only educational institutions were earlier permitted to set a community radio. The policy has been liberalized by the government with a view to allow greater participation by the civil society on issues of development and social change.

Presently, 29 Community Radio Stations are operational. Out of this, 28 institutions were granted permission under the old guidelines and one Institution viz. Delhi University was given permission.

Index

P

R

S

T

V

W